VINCIS

THE ART
AND SCIENCE
OF WINNING

About the Author

A sales professional for 28 years and a stand-up comic for 5, Nicci has a unique outlook on presentation. When she learnt sales, in a competitive, commission driven company selling IT, it was a very different world. Sales was a short process populated by aggressive, young alpha-males.

Presentations have evolved, and so has Nicci. That final 'close' is now not enough, and Nicci has found that a more nurturing, feminine approach is necessary. As sales have changed, so has she, transitioning at work to help foster a more motherly role.

VINCIS

THE ART
AND SCIENCE
OF WINNING

Nicci Take

Matador
9 Priory Business Park,
Wistow Road, Kibworth Beauchamp,
Leicestershire. LE8 0RX
Tel: 0116 279 2299
Email: books@troubador.co.uk
Web: www.troubador.co.uk/matador
Twitter: @matadorbooks

ISBN 978 1789017 526

British Library Cataloguing in Publication Data.
A catalogue record for this book is available from the British Library.

Printed and bound in the UK by TJ International, Padstow, Cornwall
Typeset in 11pt Gill Sans by Troubador Publishing Ltd, Leicester, UK

Matador is an imprint of Troubador Publishing Ltd

Confidante, mentor, supporter, coach, sounding board, realist, pragmatist, friend, mother, partner, lover, soul mate, wife: Debbie.

Vincis   **[vin-sis]**

Latin Verb

'You Win'

TABLE OF
CONTENTS

———————————

Introduction

WHY DO WE PRESENT?

When we have something important to say, we stand up, and we say it.

The spoken word and the 'in-person' presentation are the dominant media in our society. Thinking about a world without them feels bizarre and abstract. Our politicians communicate by speeches, we get our news on TV or in videos, and we teach in classrooms in person.

It isn't a surprise, therefore, that we sell in person. Every day, business people from all across the world are subjected to the same sales presentation experience. Forty to fifty minutes (which feels like hours) of the same, dull bullet points, as static as they are unmoving.

Why do we even bother with this? The simple truth is that almost all literate people can read quicker than they can be read to.

In the tedious presentation-status quo, the presenter stands up front and goes to the effort of talking, but we all ignore them. In part, we ignore them because what they have to say isn't interesting – it isn't relevant to us and perhaps their delivery isn't engaging – but we also don't listen because there's no need. If what they're saying (or something very similar to what they're saying) is already written behind them, why would we bother waiting around to hear them read it, when it's quicker for us to read ahead ourselves?

For that matter, why do politicians stand up in Parliament, or Congress, or the White House, and read their speeches to the public when they could just as easily write an editorial in a newspaper? Or write a blog post? The audience could get all of the words more quickly. Right?

This debate has raged for millennia, with Socrates – a lover of the spoken word – and Plato – one of his students, who was in favour of written argument – in conflict over which medium was the best way to convey ideas.

Personally, I don't believe that reading from a script works in business presentations. I do believe that writing a script is a valuable exercise, but learning it and repeating it verbatim is counterproductive. We coach people to write the script to organize their thoughts (Plato), then throw it away and get to their feet and practise (Socrates). As a stand-up comic, I know that scripting can be vital. Punch words have to be at the end of the joke to allow the audience 'space' to laugh. That said, rehearsing this to the point that it feels unspontaneous is counterproductive.

On the other hand, it's quicker to read, and – more importantly – reading can happen anywhere, at any time, and as many times as the reader wants. In those respects, the written word is a vital means of communication. For some things (for example, books about presentations), the written word is unrivalled.

In the UK, our political system is based on the ideas of Socrates: stand up and debate your case. And it's for a reason: written arguments, white papers, even blogs are not as persuasive or as revealing as the cut and thrust of a debate. Being able to see the presenter, being able to ask questions of them, hear their tone of voice, and, when used correctly, perhaps even benefit from visual aids, makes the spoken word a richer, fuller experience, but a pre-debate white paper can also be invaluable.

Presentations should be dynamic; text is static.

The presenter has a greater control over the experience of their audience, so is able to tailor their approach as they go. The experience provided by being able to see the presenter, to hear all the variation in the tone of their voice, even to see what they're wearing, is one that can't be recreated in print. That's why making your case, justifying your arguments and thinking on your feet is central to our political system, our education system, and, I would argue, human relationships. I agree with Socrates.

Chapter 1

THE POWER
OF POWERPOINT

I hate the way people use slide presentations instead of thinking.
Steve Jobs

Standing up and speaking in front of a group is, as was discussed before, an incredibly old medium. Over time, however, presenters have drawn on different types of visual aid. For many people, the concept of using visual aids needs no advocating; they readily accept the point that many presentations are better for including the use of some diagrams, pictures, or slides, though how well they really work is another matter.

From early on the computer revolution, many visual aid methodologies have been in decline. Though they still have their uses, 35mm slides, overhead projector (OHP) slides and even whiteboards, flipcharts and the humble blackboard, are being used less and less. For simple applications, even a handwritten note or rough diagram on the acetate of the OHP may still suit. For instance, many meetings do not involve a presentation prepared in advance, the presenter's role is as a facilitator and what is put up on screen may only be conceived as the session proceeds.

But for many, many people the ubiquitous PowerPoint™ is the method of choice when preparing a presentation and knowing that the task must include the creation of some slides. We all work at computer screens these days, and PowerPoint™ is simply one of the many applications that we must get used to; indeed, its very availability on the desk in front of us is one of the main reasons for its choice.

Why Use Technology like PowerPoint ™?

It is tempting to put the answer to this as 'Why not?' since it seems that this is sometimes the level of thought that goes into the decision to use it or not. When used properly, there are considerable benefits to using PowerPoint™, but when used inappropriately, presentations can be made much worse by it. The popular benefits of using PowerPoint ™ are that it is easy, everybody else does it (so we won't look out of place), and the audience knows what to expect.

Well, falling off a cliff is easy but that's not an excuse for doing it. 'Everybody else does it' is just as bad, and it may actually be correct that the audience expects to be abused, bored and generally disappointed, so why bother? Here's why.

Technology like PowerPoint™ will allow you to make your presentations:

- more *impressive*
- more *effective*
- more *memorable*
- more *engaging*.

A Different Approach

When PowerPoint™ arrived on the scene it held the possibility to usher in a new age. Like an industrial revolution of presentations, this new technology offered a world of potential. Now anyone could make a presentation, it was quick, easy, and cheap. This left two possible futures: a massive increase in quality, ushering in a revolution in sales, or an increase in quantity.

The release of PowerPoint™ *should* have ushered in a new age. Many people in the business world were proclaiming a new order, a new method of communication, a medium so powerful and so sophisticated it would change the way the world presented forever. It did, but the effect was not, as we hoped, for the better. Instead of the features of PowerPoint™ being used to produce simple, attractive, well-animated, and well-articulated diagrams, what we got was the bullet point, and we got it again and again and again. In fact, the only obvious difference between the old OHP acetate and the PowerPoint™ presentation was that the number of slides multiplied. There were suddenly many more of them; oh, and they were now in colour and able to move into view when the presenter was ready. What was spoken in presentations became what was read off lengthy text slides.

The promise of better communication, simpler presentations, less time assimilating information and more time debating actions has been lost in a surfeit of slides, much of it prettied up by irrelevant and often annoying clip art, or even worse, the '*I have a digital camera and I know how to use it*' school of adding irrelevant pictures.

Those of us involved in promoting the 'PowerPoint™ revolution' got one, but not the one we hoped for. Instead of improving the world's business presentations, the approach PowerPoint™ has led so many people into has made them worse. It has condemned millions of people to spend more time in their boardrooms (or should that be *bored* rooms?) watching the irrelevant, soporific, swoosh of bullets flying on screen from the left.

Too often people seem to leave common sense at the door as soon as they walk in to give a presentation. Preparation now means using PowerPoint™ to prepare the slides; it means organising the bullet points into a logical order, and presenting simply becomes an entertaining and self-congratulatory reading of the bullet points. When the presentation material (i.e. the slides) are dull and boring, then the success of the presentation depends largely on the soft skills of the presenter; if he/she is witty, passionate and enthusiastic then the audience will respond, engaging with the presenter and not the material. A different approach allows the material itself to become interesting and engaging, while the presenter's ability to entertain becomes less important. I am not suggesting that the soft skills are irrelevant, just that it is possible for people to give persuasive *or* informative presentations that are good and engaging, without being the company's best performer.

Alongside this massive emphasis on soft skills, there have emerged 'how to present' courses and PowerPoint™ training, much of which may be useful, but which seem to us to somehow miss the key point; certainly they have failed to halt the pied-piper effect of PowerPoint™.

There *is* a body of knowledge that can be applied to a presentation, some useful theory that can improve your presentation and avoid this pitfall without too much effort – it just requires you to think about your audience and learn some simple techniques for using PowerPoint™ to its best effect.

This book is my atonement – I spent years convincing people to buy data projection equipment on behalf of companies such as Proxima and Infocus, hammering home benefits that never, in fact, materialised. Having a decent laptop and a good data projector is the basic requirement of a good presentation – people *do* remember much more information if it is presented using multi-media. But multi-media is not 150 bullet points per hour, nor is it a substitute for practice and preparation.

Contained in this book are the basic techniques of a different approach to make your presentations effective. Moving away from old habits and deploying them effectively may need a change in mindset – to call it a paradigm shift is not overstating it. Armed with a projector, a laptop and some ideas from this book, maybe you can begin to break free of PowerPoint™ convention, beat the cult of the bullet point and really begin to impress your audiences.

The techniques reviewed here should be accessible to the average presenter and should improve their presentations immediately. The truly gifted presenters may discover in this book much that they do intuitively and may find it useful only as a reminder. I believe *every* reader will get something from this text and begin to use technology such as PowerPoint™ to:

- Improve communication
- Assist greater and easier assimilation of information
- Shorten presentations
- Stimulate debate
- Engage audiences without boring them.

Having heard me knocking bullet points, you will notice that they are already in use here. A book primarily *is* text, and in a book tens of thousands of words long, every graphic device that makes reading easier — paragraphs, bold type, boxed sections *and* bullet points — is worth using. This is not a failure to practise what we preach, books and presentations are different, no matter what the novel written out on some slides might suggest.

A Change of Perspective?

We all know intuitively what makes a bad presentation; we have all been abused by presenters over the years. We probably also know empirically what a good presentation is, from the audience's point of view.

Yet when we come to prepare our own presentation

our thoughts are usually not with the audience but focused on questions such as 'What shall I present?'

We write, design, and produce PowerPoint™ presentations in order to help the audience to assimilate the content of the presentation (what else is a presentation for?). We shouldn't design slides that help the presenter stay on track, or lists for the presenter to talk about; we produce images that engage the audience.

What's in This Book?

At first glance at the images in this book you may be forgiven for thinking that it is a design manual. The most obvious difference between the before-and-after examples scattered throughout these pages is principally that they have been produced by a designer.

However, turning boring dull slides into engaging presentations takes more than just design. It takes a deep understanding of communication and presentation techniques and a willingness to work at short notice against horrendous deadlines.

Producing a book that is predominantly text about a method of presentation that is predominantly about moving pictures has been a challenge. There is always the issue of being able to show you the examples we need to. To this end the book has an accompanying web site: vincis62.com/book.

On our website, you will be able access a series of web links that will show you the actual slides and, in many cases, streaming video footage that shows me presenting them.

The next issue is how to lay out the material. Most of it interlinks: how you present a slide depends on how it is designed, and how it is designed depends on how you are to present it. I hope that the interlinked nature of the material will become apparent, but since a book is not interactive I have structured it in a linear manner as best I can.

The book follows a simple structure:

- Chapter 2 addresses the current state of presentations.
- Chapters 3 – 7 explore our alternative method for presentation production and how to implement it.
- Chapter 8 looks at the different types of Presentation and how our approaches to each type differ.
- Chapter 9 addresses the role of the Presenter.

Just Another Presentation Book!

There are countless books published on the subject of presentations. All of them have one purpose; helping people stand up and deliver information with confidence and clarity. Most of these books are largely similar in nature. They talk about 'soft skills' – skills associated with personality and confidence: how to speak, how to stand, where to look, what to say, how to say it, and which visual aids to use and where.

In fact, more people are afraid of public speaking than all of the people who are afraid of large spaces, spiders and death put together. So, statistically, at a funeral more people are afraid of doing the eulogy than they are of being in the coffin! The presentation skills industry largely focuses on helping people overcome their fears, enabling them to stand up and deliver with confidence.

Having coached 10,000 presenters, my experience is that confidently speaking about the wrong things to the wrong people at the wrong time and showing them the wrong visuals isn't a good way of having an impact.

My team and I focus on 'hard skills', advice based on science and proven practice that makes audiences pay attention and, therefore, remember the context and purpose of every interaction. It's not about confidence, it's about skill, knowledge, and practice.

This is not just another presentation book. It points to a different way of thinking about presentations and, more importantly, it points to a different way of using technology. It does not replace the other books on your shelf, nor does it invalidate any of the sound advice contained in them, other than the role of the visual aid. However, by radically altering what you show your audience using tools such as PowerPoint™, you will make more use of your soft skills, improve your impact, and the audience's recall of your presentations.

At m621 Vincis our aim is simple:

We take our client from winning an average of 1 in 3 to an average of 3 in 4.

We do this through a number of techniques, all of which I'll explain in this book. This book therefore, has exactly the same Value Proposition:

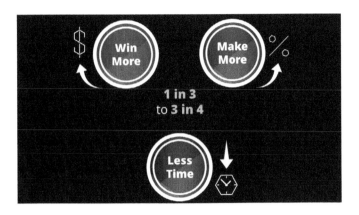

Chapter 2

PRESENTATION REALITY

It is sometimes an appropriate response to reality to go insane.
Steve Vallis

Before and After

The slides here are an example of a before-and-after for one of our clients, Bayer. The first one is a fairly standard

Background

- In the mid-1950s, granules similar to those found in endocrine gland cells were observed in endocardial cells from the atria. This was the first indication that the heart also can function as an endocrine organ.

- Scientists had searched for a long time for "Third Factor," the factor in addition to GFR and Aldosterone that controlled fluid balance.

- In 1981, a product of cardiac secretion, atrial natriuretic peptide (ANP) was first described and was subsequently shown to induce natriuresis and vasodilation. It is also an antagonist of the renin-angiotensin-aldosterone system.

- In 1988, a molecule of the same family was discovered in pig brain and was named BNP (Brain Natriuretic Peptide). This was later found to be produced by ventricular myocardial cells.

- In 1990, a third peptide, CNP, was discovered in the nervous system and vascular epithelium.

- Recently, a fourth peptide called DNP has been reported.

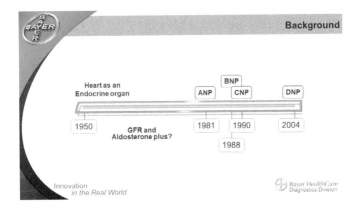

PowerPoint™ slide, the second our interpretation of the same information. We think the second slide is better.

So this is a book about how to use presentation technology– not a technical 'how to insert photo' kind of book, but a 'how to use presentation tools to create and deliver truly effective presentations' kind of book. I will go through what a 'winning presentation' is, and how to achieve one, but first let's examine the status quo.

The Worst Presentation Ever?

The worst presentation I have ever seen was at a logistics conference several years go. I was coaching a client through a 35-minute presentation on 'Technology For Warehousing' and he had the second slot on the second day of a three-day conference. Because we were second prior to the mid-morning break, we had to sit through the first presentation: 60 minutes on 'Just In Time Delivery In The Automotive Sector'. It should have been interesting enough, but the presenter, an authoritative man in his early 50s, started by handing out a copy of his slides (68 pages) and script (22 pages) and as he read his script his assistant pressed CLICK each time he moved to another bullet point.

What soon became apparent was that his script and slides were identical. He was using PowerPoint™ to put the script on screen, line by line. Within ten minutes (on slide four) the audience realised what the next 60 minutes had in store for them and decided *en masse* to go to sleep. The only engaging thing about any of his presentation was that his assistant managed to get ahead of him by two slides whilst he, head down, blindly read on – no doubt completely unaware of his snoring victims in front of him.

Death by PowerPoint™

The 'normal' approach to presentations using PowerPoint™ (30 slides, blue background, yellow text, all the same layout, a heading and five bullet points) is so prevalent, and so universally ill-received, that it has recently become the subject of considerable academic and journalistic comment and it is the slides that come in for the greatest criticism.

For instance, in America a well-known and respected academic, Edward R. Tufte of Yale, who is an acknowledged corporate communications expert, has written a strong condemnation of PowerPoint™ in '*The Cognitive Style of PowerPoint*'™ (which you can read in full by accessing www.edwardtufte.com). One fascinating example he uses concerns the Columbia space shuttle disaster. In a slide presentation – which Tufte calls 'an exercise in misdirection' – the text giving pre-flight advice was 640 times larger than the crucial piece of information about the foam section which detached and crippled the craft. It was buried in small type several layers down in a busy PowerPoint™ list. Though the danger this might pose was actually flagged, the warning was not noticed. The main heading on the slide indicated a positive outcome to tests, saying: 'Review of Test Data Indicates Conservatism for Tile Penetration'. One might criticise the language too, but the point remains – the key information was passed over unnoticed, seemingly because of the way it was presented.

Additionally, to reinforce any lingering feelings you may have that traditional PowerPoint™ style and practice are fine, try looking at www.norvig.com/Gettysburg where Peter Norvig has posted a wonderful spoof of Abraham Lincoln's Gettysburg address:

'Four score and seven years ago our fathers brought forth on this continent a new nation, conceived in

*liberty and dedicated to the proposition that all men
are created equal.'*

Such stirring language and thoughts are reduced to banality by a visual presentation that is not visual and which uses bullet points such as 'Met on battlefield (great)'. As an example of how to reduce a powerful and memorable message to insignificance, this is a classic.

The fact remains that the prevailing style of PowerPoint™-driven presentations, while they are something audiences expect and so often tolerate, do not really satisfy audiences as they should. A good, stylish presenter, with presence and panache, may be able to make up for this, but only in part. The criticism comes because this kind of PowerPoint™ use is worldwide and large numbers of people notice that it fails to do a complete job, though that might be better worded by saying that presenters allow it to do a poor job.

So are these pundits right? Is PowerPoint™ intrinsically evil?

Edward Tufte *et al* certainly have a sound argument based on what the vast majority of the world's 450 million PowerPoint™ users are doing with it. However; it is *how it is used* that causes the problem and the audience abuse. The PowerPoint™ system itself is not to blame. Transform its use and you transform its effect.

Consider a 13th century Samurai sword, crafted by someone who dedicated their life to perfection, creating a blade so sharp it can cut falling silk, so strong it can slice through trees. In the hands of the Samurai the sword represents justice, protection and a way of life based on simplicity and harmony. To many people it is a thing of beauty. Yet not so long ago in the UK such a sword was used to kill innocent passers-by, by a man clearly unhinged. Does that make the sword evil? Does it diminish its beauty or its usefulness? Clearly, it does not. PowerPoint™ is the same: just because many of its 450 million users use it badly, that does not make it a bad piece of software. It simply exposes some inadequate communication skills.

The solution is apparent: we don't need to change the tool, merely the way we use it. A change in thinking is required, that paradigm shift we have referred to. The way many people think about PowerPoint™ must change. If we reassess the manner in which we use it, and, perhaps, accept that it has its uses and its limitations, and that it is not the perfect medium for all forms of communication, it will work better for us.

The Right Look and Use

The traditional way of putting together slides together is as a list. At its simplest, this might look something like this.

Value Based Care Model

The Difference:
- Physician-directed care plan
- Enhanced access to care
- Shared decision making
- Coordinated care with other providers
- Prevention and wellness recommendations
- Extended office hours
- Recommends lower cost options that won't affect quality

Such slides, especially in such a key role have already been commented upon – savaged, if you like. There is more to say, however, to show just how powerful the approach we are describing is – and, bear with me – it starts with a rant.

The kind of slide that turns audiences off most surely is the one with the list where the extensive words are read out verbatim.

We have all seen slides with the equivalent of a short novel on them: dull, inappropriate, and likely to prompt a tedious presentation, where almost everything said is read from the screen. So what happens? Well, the slides may get used just like that, and many are, but sometimes, someone – the presenter themselves or a colleague, perhaps – admits that the overall effect looks ... *a little dull*.

C.L.I.P. A.R.T.: Crass Little Inserted Pictures Always Rubbish & Trite

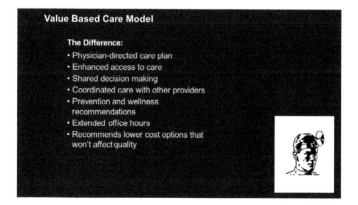

They decide something must change. So, working their computer literacy overtime, they add a little picture – fitting in a piece of clip art. This is how a slide that links somehow to the subject of meetings, perhaps describing a project and setting out the review process, ends up with a picture of a little group of brightly coloured cartoon characters sitting round a table gazing out from the bottom left-hand corner of the slide and jostling the type into odd shapes.

What a change! This is now a dull, inappropriate slide with an inappropriate piece of clip art added in, and doing nothing to rescue the situation. It does not help. People do not say 'Wow!' and hang on every word of the text just because the picture is now there. Really, they do not. The overall effect is still bland, and in many cases – certainly for something intended to be a winning slide – the creation of it is a waste of time and effort. Yet, people are curiously wedded to this style. For example, in one international organisation during a sales workshop, participants spent a day creating and making presentations, all accompanied by endless, very wordy slides. Suggestions that this might be changed were initially vehemently rejected: *it's what we always do!* Yet after some hours of being on the receiving end, and being the audience for their own style of presentations, the point was made and they raised suggestions for change.

The reason that 'visual aids' are used so ineffectively is simple: They're made with the Presenter in mind, not the Audience.

A list of bullet points is designed to assist the presenter, indicating what they are going to talk about and in what order. They serve to prompt them to remember their lines.

The performing arts phrase for this is to 'cue the presenter'.

This isn't an approach that is sympathetic to the audience, as we will explore later.

Distraction, the Presenter's Enemy

The audience can only remember that which they heard, or saw; if your listeners weren't paying attention, they will have zero retention of the information. It makes sense, therefore, to get and hold the attention of your audience. Later, we will look at the audience's attention span for this reason. Clearly then, we must allow the audience to pay attention to the appropriate piece of communication.

I will mention this several times in this book as it pertains to each section. There are four sources of distraction:

- Content
- Presenter
- Design
- Animation.

Let's look at them in turn.

Content

The biggest problem with presentations that we encounter is that they have too much information in them. Much of it is interesting, but irrelevant. This is then delivered too fast for the audience to understand much, if any, of it. The rule should be only to include information that is 100%

strictly relevant to the arguments being made. Anything less than this encourages the inclusion of information that 'may be useful' or worse 'may be interesting'. These pieces of information have a habit of distracting your listeners and, worst of all, prompting them to stop paying attention to the presentation as their mind wanders down a path inspired by an irrelevant observation.

In most sales presentations, we suggest condensing the message down into a 'Value Proposition' of only five points.

Presenter

Presenters distract audiences in two ways: either by saying something or by doing something inconsistent or irrelevant (or just plain annoying). There's nothing wrong with grabbing attention – since I wrote the first edition of this book my presentation style has evolved somewhat, through presenting with my nails painted to presenting in full 'Nicci' mode. As long as it's planned and confidently presented it can work well.

Design

If the audience walks away from the presentation discussing the design of the slides and not the message, then we have failed. The design needs to be good enough to allow the message through but not in any way divert attention. Irrelevant pictures in the background are one distraction, as are relevant pictures that can't quite be seen, prompting the audience to try to decipher the imagery.

Animation

This is the most frequently misused distraction technique. Animation can be very powerful; we use it to draw the audience's attention to where we want it to be. Animation for animation's sake, however, can have the exact opposite effect and bring the audience's attention away from what we want them to be focussing on.

Each of these areas of potential distraction is discussed in detail later on. Much of the content is simply-applied common sense. In order to communicate effectively, the audience have to be paying attention to what we are showing them and listening to what we are saying – all at the same time. The less we distract them, the more they pay attention, the more effective the presentation. What we do is not complicated, just different from the norm.

How Good Is Your Memory?

People can only remember what they paid attention to, but attention alone is not enough. Since we can't remember what we've forgotten, it's easy to imagine Long Term Memory to be perfect, but research has shown that this is far from true. (Ebbinghaus, 1885 / 2013) (Murre and Dros, 2015)

The truth is that we forget a shocking amount of the information we process in all walks of life.

The purpose of a presentation is, surely, to get the audience to remember the content. Presentations are about delivering information, usually to modify behaviour either to persuade the audience to our point of view (i.e. sell them something) or to educate them (which is less about persuasion and more about imparting knowledge). Either way we need audiences to remember the content. Presenters should care about memory. After all, if the audience doesn't remember a presentation, it can have no effect on their future decisions.

The Research

Let me start by saying I am not an academic and have absolutely no wish to pretend otherwise. My interest is in the practical application of memory research in a presentation. While I have included some references to the research that I am aware of, clearly, it needs to be read within this context: I am a presenter looking for ways of enhancing communication and not a psychology student looking to pass a mid-term assessment.

That said, memory research began with Herman Ebbinghaus, a German Psychologist, over a hundred years ago. What is clear now is that memory is a complex thing and we do not have a simple model for it. Ebbinghaus invented a series of nonsense symbols and used it to test his recall ability. He showed that memory decays over time (Ebbinghaus, 1885/2013). In the late 19th century William James suggested that there are different types of memory, one for immediate things like the last sentence you just read, and one for older memories, such as the best meal you have ever had! (James, 1890).

Winning Presentations Implication:

Audiences will remember more today than tomorrow, more tomorrow than next week. As presenters we need to be aware of this, don't assume that just because you presented information before, it will be instantly familiar to the audience.

These are now generally known as '**Working Memory**' and '**Long Term Memory**'.

We know from research done by MILLER (1956) that Working Memory is finite and probably a relatively small 7, plus or minus 2 items (see the section below on "chunking"). However, Long Term Memory appears to be infinite or, at least, very large and it is into this store that we as presenters need to transfer information. Only from here will it affect behaviour. It's worth noting that Long Term Memory has been shown to be less than exact and people have a tendency to remember things in a way that makes sense to them but doesn't actually reflect what happened – a point worth remembering!

If Miller was correct and Working Memory is 7 +/– 2, the moment you present a slide with more than 5 facts on it, you lose control over which of these the audience will recall. By limiting the information to no more than 5 facts on a slide you increase the chance of recall. The same goes for the complete presentation: more than 5 arguments or ideas and you are increasing the amount they will forget and decreasing your effectiveness.

- Five (or fewer) pieces of information on a slide,
- Five chunks of information in a presentation (or fewer).
- The more information you present, the less in percentage terms they will recall.

Memorable Presentations

I'm always fascinated by the way memory diffuses fact.

Diane Sawyer

Mnemonic processes

Active Processes

Suppose I ask you to remember the following number 4476262458404, what would you do to remember it? From a very young age both of my boys could recite my mobile phone number, and my daughter could remember the first 6 digits at 18 months. They can do this because I set out to teach them the numbers in case of emergencies. I used several well-established techniques, Chunking, Rehearsal, Visualisation, Narrative Association, and Acoustic Association, to get the children to remember it. Almost certainly you know all of these tricks. You use them every day; you were probably taught them by your parents and you will teach them to your children, possibly without even being aware of what you are doing.

As an experiment write out your mobile telephone number on a piece of paper for me and then look at what you have written, 90% of you will have just demonstrated Chunking without realising it. Look carefully at the number, did it look like this: 4476262458404 or did you do what most people do, which is this:

4476 2624 584 04?

Note the gaps. When you are on the phone ask somebody to give you their number, they will split it up for you with each section less than 5 numbers. We do it instinctively. Some people will say that it is so the other person can write it down but if that was the issue we would put a space (or pause) between each number. It is actually a reflection of how we remember the number, or, if you like, how we encoded it into our Long Term Memory.

When we do this for ourselves (for example, when trying to memorise a phone number), it is called an 'Active Mnemonic Process.' Since it is very difficult for us to influence whether or not someone employs an Active Mnemonic Process for themselves, we instead try to mimic the process in our presentations. For example, by breaking up the data into 5 logical chunks, we can pass over the data in a form that's already easy to remember. This mimicking of the Active Mnemonic Process for our audience is called a 'Passive Mnemonic Process'. It does part of the processing for the audience, which boosts recall.

Here is a brief description of some of the more prominent Passive Processes that we embed into presentations and how we can use them to improve the amount of information audiences recall.

Passive Mnemonic Processes™

Here is a mnemonic device called CRAVE that we use in presentations:

Chunking

As I described above, this is the process of structuring the information into meaningful logical chunks and then presenting it in sections. We have shown countless times that by splitting the presentation up into sections, we both increase the amount of information recall and significantly impact which information is recalled.

Relevance

This is important for two reasons: firstly, it encourages engagement, since people will pay attention to information they know or think will be of direct use to them, and secondly, people tend to remember facts more easily if they are related to something that they already know. Clearly, this is part of getting the message right but it is also about demonstrating how the information is useful and reminding the audience why it will be useful (since they are likely to forget unless you re-expose them to this fact).

While this impacts the decision to include information in the content of the presentation it also impacts the narrative, since the presenter needs to help the audience to build connections to things they already know. The best example of this is during a sales presentation, where we encourage sales people to use the Value Proposition as a questioning aid before the presentation is delivered to find facts about the prospect that can be worked into the patter of the presentation to help prove relevance.

Association

Narrative

Properly called 'Narrative Story Method,' Bower and Clark showed that telling a story to link words together causes a clear increase in recall (Bower and Clark, 1969). We use this to link ideas, such as arguments to buy, into a story that help the audience recall the benefits. For example, if the benefits of our system were Productivity, Rapid Turnaround Time, Quality results, Consistency, and Patient Care we might suggest that the salesperson uses patter like this:

> *"Our clients have told us that the use of our medical diagnostics equipment impacts their facility in five key areas, they are all struggling with staff shortages (Productivity) and at the same time need to provide their Doctors with test results quicker and quicker (Rapid TAT). These results need to be accurate (Quality Results) to prevent retesting and misdiagnosis and follow-up tests need to be consistent (Consistency) if they are to have an impact on Clinical outcomes (Patient Care)"*

But if they have the soft skills to cope then this will work better:

> *"Imagine it from the patients' point of view, once the Doctor has drawn the blood for the tests the patient*

doesn't want to be told he has to wait because the laboratory is short staffed (Productivity), he wants the results as quickly as possible to remove the anxiety of uncertainty (Rapid TAT) while he is still in the ER. The last thing he wants to hear is a misdiagnosis because of poor quality (Quality) and if this is his second visit he will want to know that the test is the same and not different because it's a different technician running it (Consistency) and finally he wants the best clinical outcomes possible, (Patient Care) wouldn't you?"

The story of a patient turning up to the Emergency Room having to wait for test results that turn out to be inaccurate and not comparable to those on his record, leading to the wrong diagnosis and treatment, will help the audience recall the five benefits. If you don't believe me try it, put the book down and relive the story writing benefits as you go, you will find you can easily recall 5 out of 5. Getting salespeople to do this is another story!

Acoustic

Honestly I can't recall using this in a presentation, but this is how my 18 month old daughter learned my mobile phone number; we sang it to her as a nursery rhyme! On the whole, it's probably better left for remembering social things rather than business facts but it is a fundamental trick in marketing slogans. Cantor, Rhyme and Rhythm will help slogans or strap lines become memorable.

Visualisation

Taking ideas, turning them into visual interpretations and combining these with the narrative, produces a very powerful mnemonic. This will be covered later in the Visualisation section.

Bower showed that by asking audiences to formulate mental images along with lists of words, recall could nearly be doubled showing 80% recall vs. 45% without these instructions (Bower, 1972). By showing the linked images you turn an active technique into a passive one. We believe you can easily show 70% recall on visualised slides vs. 15% on bullet points.

Part of the impact of this technique may be what is known as 'dual encoding' (Mayer, 2002), the brain processes visual and auditory information in different ways, and by encoding information simultaneously visually and aurally, the material can be better recalled.

Visual messages work better than oral ones, visual messages with oral explanation works better than either. However, a visual message is not just a photograph pasted into your slide, the image has to convey a specific message.

Elaborate Rehearsal

Rehearsal or repetition is a primary mnemonic process but it can be used in two ways: simple rehearsal is where we take the key messages and repeat them throughout the presentation (for example a Value Proposition wheel is shown at least 7 times in one of our sales presentations). However, it seems that simple rehearsal or "Rote" is less effective than "Elaborative rehearsal" – connecting the 5 issues with a story or a Narrative (Bower and Clark, 1969) (Craik and Watkins, 1973). This is what we encourage presenters to do when presenting the Value Proposition Wheel.

When I am teaching I use a simple exercise to illustrate how repetition can impact recall. I read out 5 numbers and then give the audience 5 seconds during which time I ask them to repeat the numbers in their head (using their Inner Voice) and then write them down. Predictably there is an average of 80% recall. We then repeat the exercise but this time we disrupt the mnemonic processing by not allowing the repetition and forcing them to count out loud from 10 down to 0 and then write down as much as they can recall. This time we get 20% recall. This exercise is called the Brown-Peterson technique (Peterson and Peterson, 1959).

If you do not allow pauses (5–6 seconds) for the audience to think about the information you have presented, they do not have time to mnemonically process the information. Therefore, they will have low recall. However, if we do pause and allow, indeed even encourage, the audience to actively process the information, then we can achieve extremely high levels of recall.

Elaborate rehearsal is essentially the key to 4 Dimensional Presenting, taking the visual information and creating an elaborate semantic repetition of it in the patter. That's not simply repeating the text on the slide but adding to it. For example, if the slide has the words "More Memorable" on it, we would actually say

"You need your presentations to be remembered by the audience after the presentation"

Thus elaborating without using the same words.

Instead of reading the text on the screen use different words to describe the same thing, this will increase the audience's recall as well as preventing the disengagement caused when somebody starts to read something that is written in front of them.

The CRAVE mnemonic is a very useful approach to the learning process.

Primacy – Recency

Murdock, using a similar technique to the number recalling exercise I explained before, managed to show that audiences are more likely to recall the first and last items in a list (Murdock, 1962).

We use this to select the order of our Value Propositions putting the most powerful first and the second most powerful last. That is unless there is a better story (Narrative Association) if the presentation order is different, in which case we assume that the story will override the effects of Recency.

Structured information

Research suggests that, in the absence of structure to information (he called it organisation), the audience creates their own (Tulving and Oslar, 1968). By providing structure to the information, the audience does not have to create their own Organisation. This frees up Cognitive Load to mnemonically process the information.

> *Give your presentations a* **Visual Structure** *to help the audience make sense of the information, thus increasing the amount that can be recalled.*

The importance of structure cannot be understated, but there are many ways of structuring information and a linear sequence is not always the most appropriate, despite the fact that the information must be presented in a linear fashion (Chronologically). We can still represent the information non-linearly visually.

This has a massive impact on the presentation. During the messaging phase of a presentation development we are looking to structure the arguments and, therefore, the information. During the visualisation stage we look to make this structure apparent to the audience.

Value Proposition Mnemonics

The most basic Passive Mnemonic Technique we use is the repetition of the Value Proposition. Value Propositions ought to have 5 elements to them (Mnemonic 1). The first time we build the slide we do so in conjunction with a narrative association to the five points (Mnemonic 2). They are displayed as a graphic producing a Visualisation of the Value Proposition (Mnemonic 3) and then repeated up to 7 times as it is used to segue the presentation (Mnemonic 4). During each section we are striving to show relevance (Mnemonic 5).

All in all the presentation works very hard to increase the chances of the audience (prospect) recalling the five reasons for buying from you rather than the competitor and it works.

Visual Cognitive Dissonance™

Humans are pattern-recognising machines.

We are quick to spot patterns where they exist and even invent them where they don't really exist (constellations in the night sky, for example). Patterns, therefore, obviously have a large impact on the way we put together presentations. Not only, as we will go into later, can patterns influence design – showing when different objects relate or don't relate to each other – the innate human desire to notice and understand patterns can also be used to boost attention.

Take the slide below;

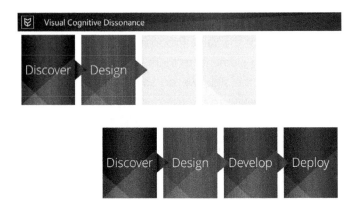

We have an expectation, that each of these boxes should look the same, and that expectation is subverted. This instantly raises the question, 'what's in the unfilled box?' Our completionist brain is now desperate to know the reason for this dissonance. Just like when we hear something unusual and clashing in music, the dissonance catches our attention. For this dissonance to be useful (again like in music) it must lead to a resolution.

The inconsistency drew our focus, and now that it's been resolved, we're also more likely to remember it. This process – of presenting something visually that doesn't make sense until the presenter explains it (either by speaking, or through advancing the slide) – is known as Visual Cognitive Dissonance™. It is a crucial part of our process. It acknowledges the audience as an active participant in the transfer of knowledge, and takes advantage of this to boost both recall and attention.

How does *Visual Cognitive Dissonance*™ impact Working Memory?

In 2012, the University of Central Lancashire, in conjunction with m621 Vincis, undertook a study to compare the effects on recall of a presentation containing Visual Cognitive Dissonance (VCD) and a 'next best alternative.' The alternative presentation was designed to be as similar to the VCD presentations as possible, with the exception of the VCD element. They used, according to the study, 'high production values, a consistent narrative, repetition and mnemonics' (Morley, A., Atherton, C. and Oulton, N. (2016)).

The study tested both immediate and delayed recall (a week after the presentation was given). Not only did the study find that VCD boosts recall, it was actually found to boost delayed recall to a level higher than the immediate recall for the next best alternative.

Obviously, the competitive implications of this are massive. VCD can allow the decision-maker to remember your presentation better in a week's time than the competition's, even if they saw that that morning.

Images that do not make sense encourage active audience engagement.

Chapter 3

WINNING PRESENTATONS

It usually takes me more than three weeks to prepare a good impromptu speech.

Mark Twain

In this chapter, I am going to explain our alternative approach to creating presentations. Fundamentally this comes in three different parts, each of which entails a different approach.

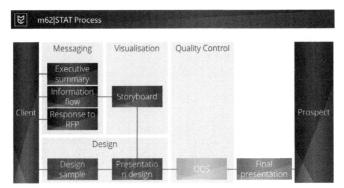

1. Messaging
2. Visualisation
3. Design

Each part of this process, however, aims to deliver the same 'winning' features, and ultimately make it a Winning Presentation. Before I go into each of these aspects of producing presentations, I'll first go through the features of a Winning Presentation.

What is a Winning Presentation?

Winning Presentations have to be Effective, Engaging, Impressive and Memorable.

Effective:

If after the presentation your audience cannot further their business goals, what was the point of the presentation?

Engaging:

If your audience isn't paying attention, what was the point of the presentation?

Impressive:

If they can discount what you said and showed them because it didn't impress or inspire them, what was the point of the presentation?

Memorable:

If after the presentation they can't remember what it was about or what you wanted them to know, what was the point of the presentation?

This book will give you the guidance you need to make your presentations win.

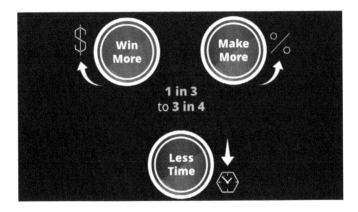

Chapter 4

MESSAGING

Setting Objectives

If you do not know where you are going,
any road will get you there.

Confucius

The first step in creating a presentation is usually to ask a simple question. 'Why?'

'Why are we giving this presentation?' This might sound obvious, but it's very easy to overlook. The biggest reason that a poor presentation is poor is that the 'Why?' question cannot be answered clearly. Without a clear intention, the presentation becomes just 'about something.' It can ramble and digress without purpose and yet still somehow be felt to be fulfilling its brief.

Thanks to this, presentations tend to have too much information and are therefore delivered too quickly.

The Purpose of the Presentation

The first thing we do when we sit with a presenter in a consultancy session is to determine the purpose of the presentation. We ask the following questions:

- What is the purpose of the presentation?
- To whom is it addressed?
- When is it?
- How long do you have?
- What do you want them to do at the end?

The answer to the last of these is probably the most important. In our experience this tells us what type of presentation we are dealing with, and for us there are only four types, each of which is covered in detail later on:

- *Persuasion* (on a rational level),
- *Motivation* (which is to persuade on an emotional level),
- *Education*,
- *Entertainment*.

All four need to impart information.

To do this they need to first gain and hold the audience's attention and then present information in the right manner, at the right time, and in the right order. Simple really!

Why?

Let us be clear. There should be no such thing as a business presentation that is just 'about something' – you always need a clear objective. Without a real objective another inappropriate and dangerous approach may become irresistible.

Faced with making a presentation, the simplest way of preparing it often seems to be starting with 'something similar'. We take the material and slides from Presentation A and adapt them to make them suitable for Presentation B. It saves time, but it is all too easy to compromise: what we end up with is a hotch-potch of slides, some suitable and others only incorporated because 'that was a good slide, John used it on Presentation C, let's build that in'. The result may certainly end up different from, and less appropriate than, what we would have created if we had started with a blank sheet of paper.

It should be a golden rule for any presenter that a clear answer can be given to the question: 'Why am I making this presentation?'

I do love the look of incredulity on the face of a salesperson when I ask this question – they usually think it's obvious – but not as much as I enjoy the one we get when they realise that 'getting the sale' is a naïve answer.

There must be a sensible reason for the inclusion of *every single element of every individual slide used* (and for the order in which they are to be used). Further, the objective for the presentation should be distinctly identifiable for the two disparate elements involved here: the presenter and the audience. Often, and unsurprisingly with sales pitches, what they want from the event is different in each case.

More presentations fail for lack of clear objectives than for any other reason. They are fundamental to success. Every management guru has their version of the maxim – 'Unless you know where you are going, any road will do'. Perhaps it is the seeming simplicity of it that can confuse. After all, the objective seems obvious; it is what it was for your last competitive presentation, to prompt the customer to buy. Right? But this just prompts the further question – how?

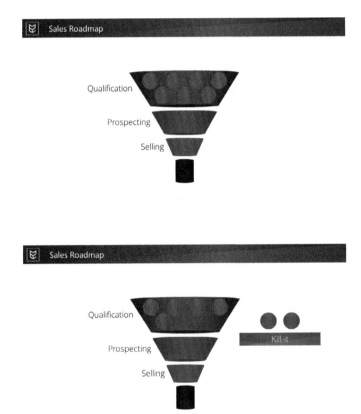

Sales Roadmap

The figure provides an effective route map. It indicates the path to success. It also shows what needs to be progressively done to align it to the audience's attention span. This is radically different from the 'me, me, me' style of presentation castigated earlier.

Can this structure really be so mechanical? Each customer, and thus each presentation, is, of course, unique, but the detailed differences always fit into the overall picture and structure described.

How do I know?

I have helped clients create over 10,000 presentations. Every one used this structure, and every client experienced an increase in conversion rates.

Approached along these lines, presentations will never seem pedestrian or 'standard'; indeed, because they are customer focused, that would be difficult. Add good delivery and good visuals, and the chances of success are excellent.

SMART objectives

A much-quoted acronym, coined by Geroge Doran, can provide a good guide here: SMART (Doran, 1981). This stands for:

- **S**pecific
- **M**easurable
- **A**ction Orientated
- **R**ealistic
- **T**imed.

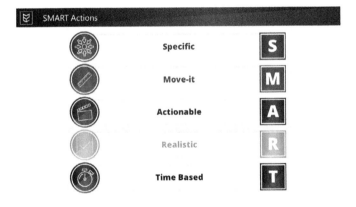

As an example you might regard objectives linked to your reading of this book as follows:

- **S**pecific: To ensure that your presentations will be appropriate and informative to your audience.
- **M**easurable: To ensure action takes place afterwards
- **A**ction Orientated: Begin making small actual steps towards changing your presentations

- **R**ealistic: The book is split up in small sections to make it easier
- **T**imed: Set aside a specific period of time, half an hour say, with a cup of coffee, and read a chapter

Formalising objectives prompts other questions and answering them focuses the objective.

How much do you want *who* to buy and *when?*

What actually needs to happen?

For instance, there is a difference between a presentation designed to persuade a known decision maker to say 'Yes' there and then, and one designed to prompt a recommendation, say from key members of the audience, to an absent decision maker. If this analysis produces a complex picture, so be it. The job is to ensure that the presentation addresses exactly what really needs to be done in all respects. Objectives are not simply important in their own right, they should assist the process of going about assembling and delivering the presentation and ensuring that it will work.

In a word, objectives are directional.

On one occasion I started a consultancy session with a salesperson pitching to keep a contract worth £6M ($8M) over the next two years. I asked about the purpose of the presentation; I was told that it was to keep the contract. The salesperson had a look on his face that clearly said that he thought this a stupid question. I then asked him, if this was the objective, who the person who signed the purchase order was, and whether that person was going to be in the room during the presentation.

It transpired that the salesperson knew who the decision maker was but he didn't know if she was going to be there. *If the decision maker was not there, how could the objective be to win the business?* Clearly this wasn't a realistic objective.

Over the next two hours we developed a strategy that culminated in him phoning the decision maker and asking her to come to the presentation. When the decision maker agreed we asked her what she wanted to see. The answer guided the presentation content and ultimately won the client the contract.

Always be clear about your objectives. It is a good discipline to write them down. It is not a chore – to be effective, you should have done the thinking that enables you to encapsulate them briefly. List what you want to achieve, what the audience want, and how they will benefit from being party to the presentation.

Ask yourself whether you are clear in this respect before you even begin to prepare. If you know *why* the presentation must be made, and *what* you intend to achieve, then you are well on the way to success. Time spent sorting this, and making sure you have a clear vision of what the objectives are, is time well spent. It may only take a few moments, but it is still worth doing. It may need more thought and take more time. So be it. It is still worth doing, and in any case it may well save time at later stages of preparation.

There have been numerous clues so far about how to structure the message of the presentation in order to maximise success. Assuming that, for the majority of readers, the success you seek is commercial, and specifically sales oriented, let's look in more detail at how to structure your presentation message to win the sale.

The art of sales is about *Feature, Advantage, Benefits*.

- **Feature**: Factual points about the product or service and the organisation selling them. For example, 'large engine and turbocharger' on a sports car.
- **Advantage**: The results of a feature. For example, 0-60 in 9 seconds for the sports car.
- **Benefits**: The potential effects of the advantages to the experience of the customer. For example, 'this can get you to work much more quickly and more smoothly.'

The core of any sales presentation needs to be about describing benefits. Most often benefits should lead the argument, after all, they're the only things that actually matter to the customer. Features and Advantages only provide a supporting role. A major problem in Messaging is the confusion of these ideas.

For all the complexities of the buying/selling process, potential customers ask themselves three fundamental questions when considering the merits of a product or service:

- **How much do I need it?** Unless what is being sold actually meets a real need, there is little likelihood of a purchase being made.
- **Can it be delivered?** Having decided that they do want it, then they have to decide that they believe the

claims being made are genuine and that the benefits being described can be delivered.

- **Is it worth it?** This is where a decision is made about value: does your Value Proposition – the overall package that you offer – satisfy the client's buying criteria?

In many cases, traditional sales presentations are quite good at this, a persuasive case is made and there is much talk of benefits. But, if no sale is confirmed, then where is the cause most likely to lie?

There is no doubt that if there is a failure, the most likely cause is that the presenter failed to create genuine *belief:* the customer is not convinced that the product is for them, is of good value and that it can/will be delivered. This principle cannot be overstated.

Attracting Attention

If what you have to say is not more
beautiful than silence, shut up.

Confucius (NT translation)

As I mentioned in the introduction, it is difficult to separate a presentation from its content. Much of what is in this section relates to presentations in general, regardless of whether they use PowerPoint™. By providing multi-media – i.e. visual and auditory information – that is harmonious, we pass information over quicker and more accurately.

Our style of presentation increases the audience's engagement and, therefore, attention – it also improves the amount of information assimilated and the accuracy of transmission. This links to a concept of 'intended message' and 'actual message' as outlined in the very useful book: *Video Applications in Business* by Hugo De Burgh and Tim Steward (Random House). By providing both streams of information we reduce the margin of error in the communication process thereby eliminating the risk that intended messages and actual messages are incongruous.

PowerPoint™ allows you to employ visual communication devices to ensure engagement and comprehension with an audience.

Attention span

If the purpose of a presentation is to transmit information to the audience with the intention of either educating or persuading them, then it is important that we understand how people retain information. We know, for example, that the amount of information learnt during a presentation deteriorates exponentially; you remember more today than you will tomorrow and more tomorrow than next week, etc. What about the amount of information actually attained during the presentation? This depends on a number of factors – not least how well it was presented – but the single biggest determining factor has to be whether the audience were actually paying attention or whether they were thinking about something else. They can surely only be expected to remember that which they actually heard, or saw.

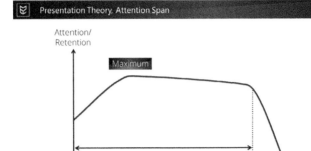

There is some research into the psychology of attention and, as we will see, it is not guaranteed. Attention starts relatively slowly, builds quickly to a plateau, and then drops away again, the final drop being somewhat sharp. The figure shows this graphically.

The time between the start of the presentation and the point at which the individual 'tunes out' is called the *attention span*.

You can measure your own by taking a stop watch and a novel, start the watch and start reading. The chances are the first time you check the watch is a good measure of your current attention span.

Even while reading this, if you watch for it you will be conscious of your mind wandering from time to time: checking the time, thinking of what you must do next, wondering if you should pause and make another cup of tea or a telephone call. This always happens, and even if what you are reading is something particularly interesting, you will still find your concentration waning. It is worth noting that women generally have a better ability to hold their attention than men (that is why girls in single-sex schools do well working at their own pace – better than girls in a co-educational environment, who have to endure the boys getting bored and disturbing their concentration).

As the figure shows, all sorts of things contribute to whether audience attention is focused on a presentation or not.

Of course, every individual's attention span varies depending on what they are faced with. For instance, it will tend to be less when they have to concentrate on something complex. It varies between individuals too – one person may be unable to concentrate on say, a television programme that fails to grip them and another easily able to see it through the hour.

While all sorts of things can affect the attention given to a presentation (even a heavy lunch or having a difficult decision to make later), some things can clearly hinder and these include:

Factors Affecting Attention Span

Presenter	Enthusiasm	Positive correlation
	Voice	Monotonic reduces attention
	Animation	Balanced
	Passion	Positive correlation
	Pace	Balanced
Audience	Intellect	Balanced
	Interest level	Positive correlation
	Opinion of Presenter	Positive correlation
	Gender	Women typically higher than men
	Age	Increases with age, flattens after teens
	Language	Familiarisation increases attention
Subject Matter	Relevance	Positive correlation
	Familiarity	Positive correlation
	Complexity	Negative correlation
	Clarity	Positive correlation
Venue	Effort to See	Negative correlation
	Effort to Hear	Negative correlation

- **The subject matter:** must be made interesting and relevant. A level of detail that reflects the audience's prior knowledge and experience with clear, easy explanation, and use of 'their language' is essential.

- **Physical barriers:** clearly if people find it hard to see or hear this creates difficulties – the venue and environment must be organised to assist the process.
- **The presenter:** enthusiasm is infectious. A clear, confident voice, varied tone and pace, suitable gesturing, and a demonstration of expertise and belief will all boost attention.

That said, consider some fundamental factors about this, and also some solutions.

Strategies to extend attention

First impressions last it is said. Certainly the first few minutes of a presentation are vital. A good start, one that grabs the attention, and that may usefully employ media such as sound, animation or video alongside what the presenter does, is a prerequisite for success. But other detailed factors help too.

You can maintain attention for longer if you read the audience and act to boost any flagging attention when necessary. There are two different techniques for doing this that we call 'hard breaks' and 'soft breaks'. Hard breaks include coffee or comfort breaks, a change of location or format. A hard break is some kind of definite break allowing the audience to think about other things (although depressingly these days it often means a 'let's check our email' break).

Soft breaks can be used more often and include:

- a change of pace
- a new topic
- variety in media
- a change of presenter or presentation
- asking a question
- examples, anecdotes and digressions (especially, if they reinforce the main theme as examples do).

After a break, continuity needs to be picked up, which may involve a summary. Once that is done, you have made a new start and attention is rekindled.

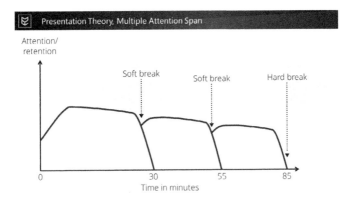

Any presentation can become dull and over-complex unless care is taken. If it is also too long or poorly targeted this will compound the problem. Prevailing standards are not so high. This creates a powerful opportunity for those determined to create a good presentation to shine – and succeed.

To add a measurable element here, we recommend no more than two soft breaks that will extend a session to 90 minutes; then a hard break is necessary.

Timing

The duration of presentations is crucial. They must not go on too long. Sales pitches last ideally 20–30 minutes and certainly not very much more, though they can, of course, lead into less formal elements and discussions. Longer events such as a training course (that might last for several days) can only be sustained by organising them into smaller segments – the kind of breaks involved here was touched on earlier.

Anticipate their attention span

Look again at the graph. You will notice that the audience typically does not pay much attention during the first few minutes of a presentation. There are principally two strategies for dealing with this. Most presentation books suggest that you employ some sort of gimmick at the front of a presentation in order to grab the audience's attention – multi-media works well, sound is compelling, or some theatre. My personal strategy, wearing a dress, is one I'd always recommend, but another alternative is to spend the first few minutes in other credibility-based activities.

Persuasion requires belief

A sales presentation must create *belief* – the way it is conducted must reflect this, it is the central bedrock of any success. To succeed you must describe value, but then you must articulate it in a way that ensures that the prospect really believes that you can deliver.

As the next figure shows there are many paths that can be taken during the sales process, but only one that leads to success. A sales presentation must present the Value Proposition and this must then be supported by a compelling case that is truly *believable*. We call this step 'justification' and it is critical. Where the sales process overall is contingent on the Value Proposition, by the time you have arrived at the pitch presentation this should be fairly solid – if not you're going to lose, whatever the presentation is like. Assuming your Value Proposition is sound, the real issue for the presentation is whether they believe that you can execute. This is where your proof of credibility is vital, whether it be social (testimonial), technical, process, or logical.

Close, Questions and Answers, Close

That done, all that remains is to ask for the order – to close (closing is another important sales technique, but beyond our brief here to deal with in detail).

Effect on Attention Span

Where does the Value Proposition fit within the total presentation?

If the Value Proposition is the most important thing, and if attention wanes if people are not rapidly engaged with what is being said, then logically it must be delivered early on. That means maybe after just three or four minutes.

However complex it may be, and however much more there may be to say about it later, the Value Proposition must come in at this stage. It must be able to be described succinctly. In doing so, we utilise one Value Proposition slide.

Think of a presentation you have made, or indeed one you plan to make. Does it have one key slide that plays this sort of role? Assuming it does, where is it placed? In a presentation using, say, 30 slides, it should not be appear for the first time further in than around number five or six. If it is much later than that, you risk losing its effectiveness; and if it is the last slide, then we would suggest you need to seriously rethink your approach.

The figure below shows the positioning of the winning slide and the following list summarises the nature of the structure we are looking at, and the sequence we believe it should follow.

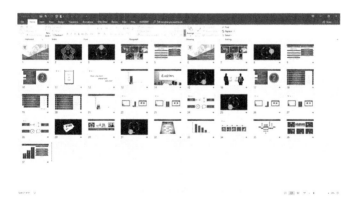

- **Introduction:** four to five minutes long establishing credibility, ending (if budget allows) with a piece of media to ensure attention.
- **Value Proposition:** a description of all of the benefits that are on offer to the prospect. This is usually five headings surrounding the title 'Why us?'
- **Proof Points:** taking the five elements of the Value Proposition in turn and offering proof of their need (if necessary) and proof of your ability to execute (essential).
- **The close:** ask for the order.
- **Question and answers:** these often delay a response to any initial close and must be dealt with effectively to reinforce belief; they are an important – and usually expected – part of any sales pitch.
- **The close:** ask again for the order.

The Winning Element

So how do you encapsulate the core message about what you offer and construct the winning slide?

The first step is to go back to basics and analyse the situation 'with a blank sheet of paper'. Nothing can be decided, much less put over in a presentation, until a clear idea exists as to exactly what stands the best chance of prompting a positive buying decision. Not only is this information crucial, but in most cases it must also be easy to express. The core message must be there, understandable and powerful, but must not take forever to present and articulate.

The process we use for identifying a Value Proposition is this:

1. Brain storm.
2. Delete irrelevant or inaccurate.
3. Collapse redundancies.
4. Rank according to customer need.
5. Rank according to competitive advantage.
6. Select best 5.

The purpose of this is as much to gain agreement about the common message as it is to find the best Value Proposition. The process usually takes about an hour with a client one-on-one, depending on our familiarity with the client's products, and can take a day in a workshop setting with all the key decision makers from an organisation (longer if you involve salespeople – all of whom generally want their say!).

We will digress for just a moment. The technique to use here is the one that takes a feature and follows it with the words, 'which means that …' For example, if a catering equipment company makes a flat grill unit for use in restaurants and hotels, they might describe a particular model as having a cooking surface of 800 square centimetres (which is clearly a feature). But this is easily transformed:

'This model can cook six steaks or a dozen eggs at once and will be just right to help cope with the rush you said always occurs at breakfast time'.

This is a good example because, whilst few people can probably instantly and accurately imagine 800 square centimetres in their mind's eye, it is certain that any restaurateur will be wholly able to imagine the description of what it will do, and see how it can help.

The So What? Game

Every salesperson will tell you that they understand the difference between a feature and a benefit. They will also tell you that they always discuss benefits with clients and never features. In my experience I cannot remember a situation where I have had only benefits in the answer to the question: If I was a prospect 'Why would I choose you?' (Alarmingly the most common response to this is 'We are cheaper.' This is perhaps the most obvious example of weak sales. Bad salespeople sell on price, good salespeople sell on value.)

There seem to me to be a number of reasons why the responses we get are often features not benefits; the first is language. By this I mean that the presenter is so familiar with the benefit behind the feature that talking about the feature automatically makes him think of the benefit.

For example, we used to use 'more impressive' as a *benefit* statement, but if we are to be analytical this is actually a *feature* of our service – the benefit is actually 'audiences frequently confuse an impressive presentation with an impressive organisation, so having a really impressive presentation can help you win more business.' The benefit here is winning more business, the feature is an impressive presentation. The fact is that it's often much easier to express features than benefits. That's no excuse, however.

My role as the outside consultant in these discussions is not to offer advice as to what the benefits may, or may not be, but simply to ensure that the audience see clearly the benefit and that this is not hidden by fogged thinking or imprecise language. The trick to doing this is by asking a series of stupid questions, to be precise a series of questions that more often than not appear to be inane, but that actually force the presenter to think through their sales logic.

By asking 'So What?' after each response to the initial question above we usually get to the benefits relatively quickly, for example:

'Why would I choose you?'
'Our equipment is faster than the competitors'.'
'So What?'
'Having quicker equipment means you can increase productivity.'
'So What?'
'Well it's difficult to get trained staff these days, so improving the productivity of the existing staff is the single biggest challenge to most of our prospects today.'

The benefit here is increased productivity, not speed.

We call this exercise 'The So What? game' and it is very useful although, be warned, it can make you unpopular or – worse – appear stupid. Let's look at one of our clients as an example.

Our client, a large IT firm, was pitching the Canadian national government for a contract to do with trade and customs. The initial information we were given was muddled, with various examples of how their technology had been deployed mixed in with the Value Proposition.

Ultimately, we helped them distill their message into the answer to two questions:

- Why do the project?
- Why do it with us?

We went through their original sales presentation with them, and took out all the important value points, creating a simple Value Proposition:

1. 2020 vision
2. Trade Transformation
3. Adopt
4. Adapt
5. Grow

There are three reasons why we advocate five points:

1. Five is approximately the maximum number of points that can be remembered
2. Three relevant points must be remembered to maximise persuasiveness of a Value proposition. If we use fewer than five, with imperfect recall and the potential that not every point is persuasive to all audience members, we may not fulfil that criterion.
3. Using five points allows the optimum time to be taken for each point whilst still keeping the presentation short enough for attention span purposes.

All this makes our 3C's of Value Propositions:

- Consistent – to boost recall
- Concise – to maintain attention
- Compelling – to actually convince the audience

We would usually create an infoflow, which is the output from the Messaging process. It aims to contain all of the information, both value and proof points, needed to begin the storyboarding phase.

The IT example below looked like this:

Presentation Information Flow
m62 vincis

Client	It Firm	Pitch	Canadian Government Pitch
Report Date	30 June 2018	Pitch Date	10th September 2018
m62 Consultant	Nicci Take	Contact details	+44151 259 6262 nicci@m62.net

Information Flow: This document is designed as a high level summary of the arguments we intend to get across to the audience in the presentation. Its purpose is to show 'what information' in 'what order' should it be presented to achieve the presentation objectives

Why do the project?
Full implementation will:

1. Provide a modern interface to trade into Canada
2. Increase speed and consistency of information processing
3. Improve the ease-of-use of the importing process
4. Eliminate repetitive information requirements
5. Target intervention and supports for Trade Chain Partners

Large transformational programs require partners who believe they can accomplish a huge goal, together. They need to understand how to operate and deliver for these kinds of programs bringing global large project experience and not just transformation consulting experience but actual business transformation experience. Throughout your RFP you outline many requirements, which we have summarized in a high-level vision:

Why us?
1. 2020 vision
2. Trade Transformation
3. Adopt
4. Adapt
5. Grow

2020 vision
"Completion by March 2020." Seeing this as a technical project will not ensure success. The project requires both an understanding of what the trade community needs today and what Canada and the community need for the future. As this solution is deployed, careful attention needs to be paid to designing a business solution that protects the border but also frees up trade. Understanding the implications both technical, commercial, organizational and legal will be required to navigate success.
There is huge scope to rethink the processes and systems that may allow innovation in to enhance both the security, revenue collection and efficacy of the system.

Trade Transformation
"This project needs to enable trade." Execution is imperative and experience shows that the technical implications are less of a challenge than the behavior change needed both internally and externally. You need to transform the way the border is managed and the secret to this is big data. Capturing it at the border and then using analytics to drive the decisions about solution design and subsequent modification will be essential to long term success.

Adopt
"It doesn't matter how good the technology is if it isn't used!" You need to drive adoption and that requires good, early stakeholder engagement. You need to involve the trade community in the solution design and then manage the adoption to drive the benefits.

Adapt
The nature of trade is changing and so too must the systems that support it" Canada needs to be easy to do business with and attractive for investment. That requires an understanding that the solution will need to adapt and change to suit the needs of the stakeholders, thus becoming a continued enabler of trade.

Grow
The ultimate goal is to increase Canadian GDP that requires a weather eye on global trade trends and a focus on growth." You need a partner who has the ecosystem that can help drive Canada's place in the G8.

Presentations have evolved: *have yours*?

The Single Most Common Presentation Error

In my experience the most common mistake made by presenters is to present too much information too quickly. It is a mistake I have made and will, I am sure, make again. Once we have defined the objectives we need to ensure we only present information that is strictly relevant to achieving the objectives and not cloud the issues by adding partially or wholly irrelevant information.

The Importance of Proof

Whatever type of information you wish to convey, whether you are operating in a commercial capacity or an educational one, whether you are selling, teaching, or lecturing, the most important thing you need to consider is how effective your presentation is going to be.

Every presentation has a purpose, either to help people learn or to help them make a decision. The more effective the presentation, the better you reach your objective of imparting the information that moves the audience on in the required direction.

I've been thinking about the benefits to teachers or trainers of making their presentations more effective. Clearly for sales people it's about winning more business, more profitably with less effort, but what about if you are not selling?

I know, it's a strange concept for someone like me who finds it difficult to open her mouth without pitching something, a project, an idea, or a joke but its true, some people want to teach.

So why would you want your presentations to be more effective if you are teaching

- Reduced time and effort – students will need things to be explained to them fewer times and more quickly
- Increases Student Satisfaction – Probably the most important metric in terms of long-term engagement and attracting more students
- Improved overall education quality – students will know, remember, and understand more, allowing them to get better exam results and advance the field.

The best lecture I have ever attended took place in September 1987. Professor Smith at Nottingham University gave a lecture on the Normal Distribution curve. I know what you're thinking: 'it doesn't sound like the most captivating topic.' I didn't want to go either, but he started by having an orderly bring an armchair into the lecture theatre and said it was for later (Visual Cognitive Dissonance ™ at work dear reader, we all listened). Then he said he had two proofs to show us. He proceeded to show us a premise and through a process of Induction and six chalkboards of equations he arrived at the proof, and wrote a large QED next to it. "E*t voila*," he said, 45 mins into a 50 min lecture.

"Everybody got that?" he said, rubbing out all but the first and last lines.

"And now for proof number two. For this you will need an armchair," he pointed, "*and a large brandy,"* which he revealed from under the counter.

He sat in the chair took a sip of brandy and said, *"After an hour or so of contemplation like thus you will in actual fact discover that the conclusion is entirely obvious. Class dismissed."*

I was so impressed. It made me think that the question

'So why would you want your presentations to be more effective if you are teaching?'

Is the wrong one. It should be:

Why *wouldn't you* want your presentations to be more effective if you are teaching?

And the answer is:

"After an hour or so of contemplation like thus… you will in actual fact discover that the conclusion is entirely obvious… class dismissed."

One important factor in influencing the level of effectiveness of your presentations is that of proof.

2,300 years ago, Aristotle wrote that, in order to persuade an audience, a speaker needed to provide proof. In fact, the most persuasive of speakers employed three different types of proof. *Ethos,* which is personal credibility, *Pathos* an emotional argument and *Logos* which is a rational argument. We find the same thing when we are writing presentations for clients; we even often follow the same order.

- **Credibility.** Sell yourself, your company and then your product in that order.
- **Empathy**. Show an understanding of the audience's needs, desires or issues.
- **Rational.** Here's why you should act, here's evidence that acting will work.

The mistake we find more often than not is an over reliance on credibility. A presentation that lasts 45 minutes should not dedicate 44 minutes telling the audience how great the presenter's organisation is. If you, or your organisation, are particularly credible, that should come through quickly. You can then dedicate the rest of the time to engendering empathy and making rational arguments.

A more effective structure, particularly for Business-to-Business sales presentations might be the following:

- Who are we?
- What do we do?
- Why do you need it?
- Why do you need it from us?
- Can I have your business?

The credibility comes in the first section and usually fits on one slide. "What we do" is not normally a service description but more a results description (In the case of my company '1 in 3 to 3 in 4' works better than 'produce PowerPoint presentations'). Then the presentations become about the audience not the presenter. Ethos followed quickly by Pathos concluded with Logos.

We find presenting the emotional argument prior to the rational argument more effective. People are inclined to look for evidence to support those things that they've already decided emotionally. Back at Nottingham University Professor Smith grabbed our emotional attention with the armchair (Pathos), established his credibility by taking us through the entire logical argument (Ethos and Logos), then finished where he started – with the armchair, this time enhanced with a brandy (Pathos and Logos)

Chapter 5

VISUALISATION

───────────────

One picture is worth ten thousand words.

Frederick R Barnard

(So why do we use a thousand words and one picture, usually an irrelevant pie chart, in our presentations?

NT)

Audience Focused not Presenter Cued

Most presentations are written to help the presenter present. They are characterised by the question, 'What do I need to present?'

This is, fundamentally, a selfish approach. Anyone whose approach to sales relies on making things as easy as possible for the salesperson is unlikely to see any success.

Winning Presentations, on the other hand, are written for the audience. They are characterised by the question,

'What does the audience need to see?' The typical list of bullet points that the presenter first develops helps them with their script. It can give the presentation structure and form and to this end it is beneficial, but it cannot prove as helpful to the audience. In fact, it can be argued that it distracts the audience, allowing them to disengage. The self-explanatory text on typical slides can be read, and if the meaning is obvious the audience member can then choose to ignore the presenter.

A list of bullet points is, therefore, best called a 'cue-card' as it cues the presenter and prompts them to talk. Winning presentations don't have any cue-cards as they add no value. We refer to the process of converting a cue-card into an audience-focused presentation as '*Visualisation.*'

There needs to be a shift from designing slides that remind the presenter what to say, to slides that help the audience understand the message.

Presentations can be approached in a different, more imaginative way that ensures they are well-focused on their chosen audience. They maximise the visual elements so the visuals truly drive the process of satisfying the audience and achieving objectives. When prevailing standards are bland, then the opportunity to shine – and create a competitive edge – is very high.

The process of achieving pertinence and impact is largely common sense, but it is also precise and it needs to be approached systematically. Certainly, at the outset it must be acknowledged that it may, initially at least, take a little longer to implement this approach than the more traditional way. It is, however, well worthwhile.

Sales presentations and pitches are often the culmination of a long sales process. When, after months of marketing, promotional and public relations activities (all of which take time and money to set up and carry out), you have the opportunity to sit in front of a client and present, the last thing you want is for the final presentation to be the weak link. If the presentation fails, then the whole process must be repeated, and the costs and time expended multiply. Countless emails sent, meetings held, and proposals written are wasted.

Time spent increasing the odds of a presentation doing what it is intended to do is time well spent. Yet, experience shows this common sense principle is often ignored. Again and again, people finish a presentation wishing they had done something to make it stronger, realising too late the chance and reward it potentially offered may not be repeated.

Presentations need to be set up and delivered correctly. If that takes time and effort, even for an experienced presenter, so be it. Accepting that, it is still necessary to know how to go about it. This is what we turn to next.

A Winning Formula

A picture really does paint a thousand words; certainly, it does a better job of communication than words alone.

Let us add to this by suggesting a short test you can try out yourself. In the first chapter of this book we showed three slides with bullet points aimed at demonstrating what factors produce a good presentation. All featured the same six points. Without turning back the pages, how many of the six points can you remember, having read them only a few moments ago? Think about it for a few seconds and write down those you can recall.

People can often remember only one or two points, despite the fact that we are talking about a time span since they saw them of not more than two or three minutes. The exception to the rule are the highly analytical people in the audience who habitually write everything down from the screen (about one in 50). The interesting question to ask these people is how much they can remember of what was said around the bullet points. The answer is usually not very much: they were not listening, they were writing! It shows that the first two of those slides were in a form that is of more use to the presenter than the audience; they provide the classic cue as to what to say. In our experience from training workshops, an audience will typically remember only 15–20% of their content.

Now think about the fourth slide (still resist turning back). This was the diagram that defined the nature of a good presentation and around which the patter that would accompany it at a real presentation would be hung. How well can you remember that? Can you sketch it out? At seminars almost everyone in the group can do that. Normally more than 95% of the audience have perfect recall of the graphic shown at the end.

What is more, they find that having the diagram in mind enables them to explain to someone else the concepts that were expressed to them.

I have been using this diagram to explain this point for twenty-five years and a couple of years ago a guy on a plane recognised me and said that I had changed the way he presented. I asked him how and he drew this diagram. The question is then simple: what would you rather have, a series of bullet points that cannot be recalled minutes after you have used them, or a series of diagrams that not only can be recalled, but can also change behaviour?

Let us look at some statistics from the psychologists again. Classic bullet point presentation result in the audience taking in 80% of the message from the presenter and 20% from the visual aids. But retention is, as we have discussed, a problem. They will only remember 20–30% of the message, even just a little later and we all know this will be less still after just one day (Bower, 1971).

The case being made is for a different vision and use of PowerPoint™ that reflects this truth. In the old way, a presenter is lucky if members of an audience remember one in four of the points made whilst a true multi-media presentation may well achieve fully three quarters of the message being retained (Paivio, 1986).

Think about what that means in a sales situation. Most purchasing decisions are not made during a presentation, they are made later (sometimes *much* later). The truth is purchasing decisions aren't made on the content of the presentation; they are in fact made on only what's remembered of that content.

Is a positive buying decision more likely to be made on around a quarter of the content of the case you made, or on three quarters of it?

Obviously, this depends on the content of the Messaging, your audience remembering more of a bad message is not going to help. However, if the Value Proposition is strong, remembering it will undoubtedly increase success. What we are setting out here might almost be described as something that gives you an unfair competitive edge.

In reality, information presented comes in two forms: what you see and what you hear. If the right patter is added to visuals that are genuinely striking and which fit well with the way people want to take information on board, then presenting is actually easier to do. It may also be more satisfying – more fun even – because it is always better to be doing something you can clearly detect is going well, rather than something accepted on sufferance.

Remember, too, that in judging sales presentations, the style is used by the audience to assess the seriousness of intent. Will the audience see a professional approach, communicating competence and trustworthiness, if the presentation is put over in a lack-lustre way consisting largely of reading lengthy text slides? No. The good presentation earns the attention it gets and then benefits from that, not only in terms of having its content appreciated, but in terms of being thought well-prepared. It is a useful bonus if, amongst the comments you get, are ones such as: '*That was very professional … They went to some trouble over that*'.

A presentation with clear objectives, put across by a presenter who has originated the visual and verbal aspects together, which works to create a strong case in a novel way and one which people see and hear so that they retain the maximum amount of the content in their minds – is a winning formula.

Pacing Information Flow

Glance at the graph below for two seconds only and then read on. How much information did you get from the quick glance? The answer is probably not a lot. Now study it for as long as it takes to work out what it is trying to say. It took longer than two seconds, but you assimilated more information. Every reader will have looked at the graph for a different length of time.

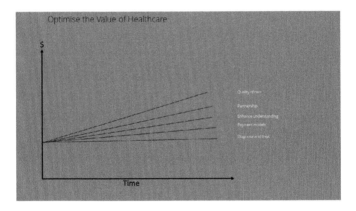

If information is printed (we call this '2D presentation') and given to an audience, the pace of information flow is controlled by the reader – they can pause to reflect or even put it down and come back later. Ultimately, the audience dictate the speed of information flow. For example, consider this book, have you read from the start of this book to here uninterrupted? Probably not. Have you read every word printed in this book from the start to here? Again, probably not (don't worry, I'm not offended).

In a presentation it is the presenter who controls the pace not the audience; the presenter decides when to click to the next slide, often regardless of the audience. There are, therefore, three characteristics that give our presentations impact: the first is the limited amount of information, the second is the strictly controlled pace of information flow, and the third is that it is laid out in order to assist assimilation.

Now look at the next sequence, the images appear and the patter is typed next to each build:

'What I am about to show you is Moving Annual Totals (explain if necessary) for the organisation for the last 18 months. The scales here show zero to plus $1,000 million.'

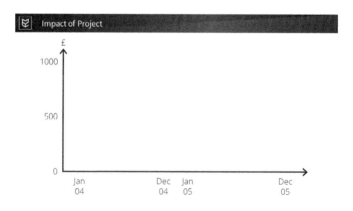

CLICK

'Look at the revenue projection before we factored in the influence of the project .'

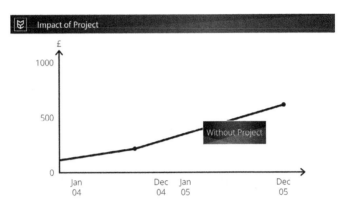

CLICK

'Now look at our actual MAT figures'

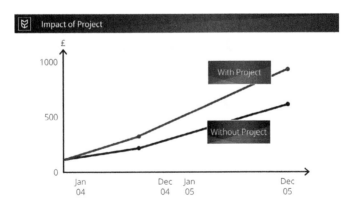

CLICK

'The impact of the project was therefore this area here…'

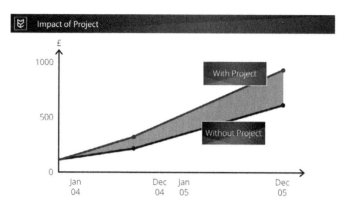

The example above can be seen presented by following the link: www.vincis62.com/book/informationflow.html

What was the difference?

Less information presented at the right speed to ensure assimilation. The ability to design a slide so as to ensure a smooth presentation of information is a core skill.

This idea applies to any slide, text only, graphs like the example above, or any of the visual devices discussed later in this section. We are not treating the audience as if they were stupid; we are simply ensuring communication (the purpose of presentation).

The reason that most presenters present information too quickly is understandable: they have seen the information before, perhaps hundreds of times, and they have had considerable time to reflect upon it and draw conclusions. The audience has not. This is probably the first time they have seen the information, so it must be presented at a pace they can cope with, not the pace the presenter chooses. By building the slides with this number of CLICKs we force the presenter to present correctly.

Four Dimension Presenting

Two-dimensional presenting describes the use of a static image or text. This is most easily exemplified by reference to a slide, which is both shown on a screen and printed out as a hard copy: if the two versions appear the same and no information is lost then the slide is 2D.

In effect, we have two additional dimensions to consider. The third dimension is time. We have the ability to modify the image over time; for example, the graph can grow or change as the presenter builds the slide.

The fourth dimension is narrative (or patter). We have the ability to explain what the audience are seeing as the image changes.

As this slide is animating, the presenter explains what the audience is seeing. The motion is compelling and almost all of the audience will pay attention and most will remember the points made because they were watching closely and paying attention.

This method of presenting is very powerful. It is engaging. It enters short-term memory and, therefore, can enter long-term memory. It is also impressive. We believe it is the way we will all present in the future.

The concept of presenting information visually links to a very specific idea, one that is behind the look and working of virtually all the slides we use and recommend. We call this 'four dimensional presenting' (4D). This is probably one of the most powerful concepts in this book. It is also the most difficult to articulate in this medium as, by definition, this book is a 2D presentation so, while this is shown here as far as is possible, the web link will allow you to see the 4D versions of the examples used here more effectively:

www.vincis62.com/book/4Dexample.html

Multi-media not Dual Media

- Dual Media – Transmission of information by two different channels (e.g audio and visual) at the same time.
- Multi-media – Transmission of information through one channel that integrates more than one medium.

Presentations have been dual media for a long time. The value of this, on the surface, is obvious; compare the experience of watching television and listening to the radio.

However, the presenter (who delivers in an audio medium) and the presentation (which is visual) can often act separately. This means that they compete for attention, distracting the audience and reducing retention. It would be like watching a silent movie at the same time as listening to an unrelated radio programme.

In true multimedia presentations, we see a seamless

interaction of two separate streams of media, merging to form a continuous flow of information using sight and sound from the presenter to the audience. The visuals are designed to be presented (and don't work without this integration) and the presenter is trained to interact with them. This is what makes for effectiveness, with the audio and visual interacting in a complementary way (increasing retention and attention from what they would be if either medium was used alone). This is like going to see a movie, complete with sound, each medium adds to the overall experience.

A good example of this can be seen by watching BBC current affairs programmes. The images and the narrative are blended seamlessly creating a steady flow of multi-media information. At the other end of the scale, try watching Fox. This is not nationalistic pride (most communication professionals would acknowledge the BBC as being the standard for broadcast media) but just a comment on what actually works. Fox have a continuous stream of headlines running across the bottom of the screen and generally too much information on the screen at any point in time. The result is that you get far less from it than from the BBC.

The elements that are involved here in producing a multi-media style include:

- Diagrams
- Animations
- Photographs
- Flow Charts (These are very useful and produce order

where order is important. They should always be used progressively, adding each element as it is discussed and highlighting the part that is being discussed as the overall picture becomes more complex.)

- Video

More information on these key elements is contained in the visual devices section of this book.

However, care must be taken with multi-media nonetheless.

One of our early clients was a famous camping stove manufacturer. The MD was hugely passionate about his products and after we had taken the brief for the presentation he showed me some video he wanted to include. The video footage was a 60-minute documentary about a team of mountaineers climbing one of the world's tallest mountains. During the black and white film there was a great shot of the company's equipment being used to boil water. However, where I wanted to include 30 seconds of the video, the MD wanted all 60 minutes. While 30 seconds of good well-shot video that makes an important point is worth the effort, it is highly unlikely that the audience share the same passion for the subject as you. Your enjoyment of footage isn't enough to justify including it; only use enough to support your argument.

Slides should be non self-explanatory

Slides that do not present an instant message create intrigue. They then help the audience to visualise the argument, encouraging the audience to pay attention. By increasing their engagement with you, you make it more likely that they will retain more of the message for longer. In this way what the presenter says – *patter* – becomes an integral part of the overall flow of information: a seamless part of the whole. Like this, we integrate Visual Cognitive Dissonance into the Visualisation phase.

Sound

If you are using animation – either PowerPoint™ animation (building a slide, etc.) or embedding some external animation (movie or flash file) – then ten seconds of silence is acceptable. More than this will become uncomfortable for the audience. You can extend this by adding sound – usually music – to around 90 seconds. Longer periods of self-running animation need either narrative or interaction, both of which start to step out of the realms of presentations and into the realm of video production.

We rarely use sound during a presentation, perhaps the occasional customer quote, but this works better as video. Sound really needs to be accompanied by something happening on screen, either an animation or a build. As soon as music starts the audience will look at the screen, and if there is nothing there they may disengage.

Photographs

There is a danger that photographs can become CLIPART– they *must* be relevant.

One of the biggest mistakes we see with photographs is poor composition. For example, look at the next three slides:

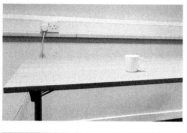

The first shot (top left hand picture) is a photograph of a mug, which has been poorly composed. The second (bottom left) picture is better (actually they are the same photograph but the second one has been cropped using PowerPoint™'s picture toolbar). The third (right) has been re-shot with better light and the picture then cut out in Photoshop™. Photographs display a massive amount of information – sometimes too much. It is often better to eliminate the unnecessary visual information and draw the audience's attention to the bit of the picture that is relevant.

Size

The next biggest mistake when using photographs is to insert excessively high-resolution pictures. There is no quicker way to increase your file size than to insert 5Mb pictures. PowerPoint™ creates slides at 72dpi (equivalent to 960 v 720) and so inserting pictures at a higher resolution than this is unnecessary and will slow the presentation down. Images should be resized before being inserted into PowerPoint (since most cameras take high resolution photos now). In general, we recommend the following sizes:

- Small images (less than half the slide) = 500pixels
- Medium images (half the slide size) = 1000pixels
- Large images (full screen image) = 1500pixels.

Maps

Maps are a great visual device, they can display a large amount of geographical information without needing to dwell on tedious details (a rare example of a situation in which information flow is too slow, not too fast).

Screen Grabs

We tend to use screen grabs a lot, particularly in technical presentations; clearly, the *Fade*, *Zoom* and *Highlight* techniques are extremely useful here. Overleaf you will see an example of a screen shot from one of our US clients, Nvoi. Since the product is a web service they have to show screen grabs. The process is easy: browse to your required screen and press the *Print Screen* key (usually 'Prt Scr'), then switch to PowerPoint™, and Paste.

However, there are some issues with this, especially if you intend to zoom in. *Print Screen* (or any other method of screen capture) will only capture at whatever screen resolution

you are running. The first trick is to increase your screen resolution on the PC and make the image as large as possible (Full Screen). This is rarely enough. We then paste this into photoshop and re-size it in 3 different sizes to keep the file sizes of our presentations down. We save the larger image with 1500 pixels as its biggest size, this is so that it'll still look great quality full screen. The next size down is 1000 pixels, this is for larger images shown on our presentations. The final size is 500 pixels, which is used for standard sized images on a slide.

Visual Segue

To *segue* means to effect a smooth and unhesitating transition from one stage or area to another.

In the context of presentations, this concept is very useful. A segue slide represents a clear break in topic within a presentation. This allows the audience to conclude their thoughts about a previous theme and prevents them from trying to connect two unrelated slides in their mind. They can also function as a soft break, extending the audience's attention span.

Introduction

Structure is important to the audience as it helps short-term memory; they feel comfortable and know where they are in the presentation. This is best done with non-verbal communication. Hence the visual segue.

We use the visual segue to move through the presentation but we also use it within the slides. Titles have to be visually different from the body text, usually a complete contrast. This involves using a graphic we call a 'Title Bar' under the titles to allow the text to be contrasted. We then use this title bar to alert the audience that the slide title has changed by having it disappear with the last slide, animate in, followed by the heading. This animation drags the eye to the title bar, making sure that the audience notices that the slide title has changed and reads the new one.

Insert Title

Title Bars

Although linked to its template by design, the title bar is eye catching and contrasting. Its job is to draw attention to a new topic. It does this by animating in prior to the heading changing. It does not animate on every slide, only on the slides where headings have changed. This alerts the audience to the change of heading and compels them to read the heading. Please view this animation at: www.vincis62.com/book/ titles.html

Graphs

Unfortunately, graphs are sometimes added not to support an argument or make a point, but to spice up an otherwise boring presentation. Presenters using bullet points often insert graphs simply to break the monotony.

Graphs should be used either to aid understanding and comprehension, or to offer proof of a point, sometimes adding credibility. Edward Tufte's (see earlier reference)

biggest complaint about PowerPoint™ (or 'slide ware' as he refers to it) is that computers often cannot show the resolution to depict accurately the true data. In this assertion he is correct, but, to my mind, he misses the point of a presentation: we are not trying to show the entirety of the data, just explain our conclusions from it.

Often, we will see graphs that simply have far too much data in them to be effectively presented. Remember the comments earlier about the pace of information flow. On paper in 2D we can show lots of data and let the reader interpret it themselves, in a presentation we cannot. In fact, we *should* not. The purpose of a presentation is almost always to *share our* conclusions, not to allow others to draw their own; there is too little time in a presentation to form opinions based on data. The data is mostly used to add weight to the presenter's argument.

To this end we invariably want to remove data from a graph in order to allow the points we need to make to be clearly seen.

There seem to me to be several different things that graphs can successfully illustrate. They can be used to show:

- Increases or decreases
- Two data sets merging or diverging
- Changes in trend.

These comparisons, alongside the concept of 'pace the information flow', have led us to adopt the following sequence for animating graphs that show comparators:

1. Animate axes, then explain them.
2. Add the first data set, describe it.
3. Add the second data set, describe it.
4. Add the comparator, make your conclusion.

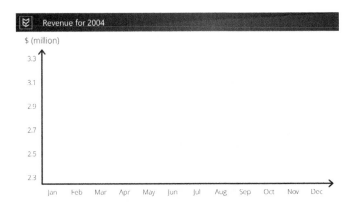

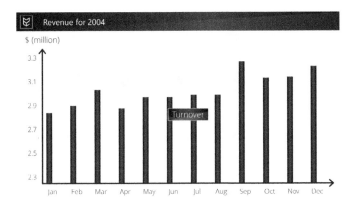

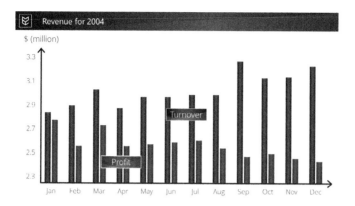

Here is a sequence that makes the point well:
www.vincis62.com/book/graph2.html

The right graph for the right purpose

A great variety of graphs and charts can be produced at the click of a mouse. Each must be well chosen.

Pie Charts

These show the relationship of a part to the whole, i.e. a proportion. This is ideal for showing, for example, the breakdown of a company's turnover by sector, but not for showing revenue growth year on year. Clearly this is best actually seen animated and can be viewed at:
www.vincis62.com/book/pie.html

Line Diagrams

These are best used to show a trend.

Scatter Plots

This type of graph is great for showing statistical analysis, but difficult to use well in a presentation.

Bar Charts

Bar charts are best used if we are to compare two sets of data. To see the whole slide build follow:

www.vincis62.com/book/bar.html

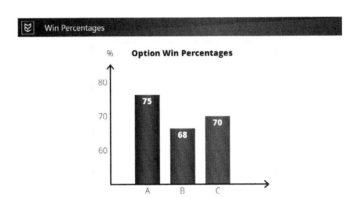

Importing Excel™ Graphs

This is possible and, provided the Excel™ file is with the presentation, any changes in the data can be updated to the presentation. However, we do not use it that often. We typically want to animate the graph according to our Objective Quality Standards and this is tricky on linked graphs. We normally recreate the graph from scratch using PowerPoint™ shapes. This makes them easier to manipulate.

Ordered Lists: Flow Chart

There are two types of flowchart, linear and iterative. Generally, if a list has an order to it (i.e. you can number it or it runs chronologically) then it will look better as a flow chart. Linear flows have a start and an end, iterative end where they start. Linear flows should ideally be laid out left to right (in the West) or top to bottom (there is more space left to right because of the aspect ratio of the screen). Iterative ones should work clockwise. Please see: www.vincis62.com/book/flowchart.html

In the West we tend to let our eye fix on the top left-hand corner of the screen, move right then diagonally down to the bottom-left, and then across to the bottom-right. It is the way we have been taught to read and is, therefore, almost reflex. The same is true on a large screen. If what you want the audience to see is not in the top left-hand corner, then you need to manipulate their focus. We have several techniques at our disposal.

Directed Attention

The idea behind 'directed attention' is to make the slide animation, the patter, and the visual cues given by the presenter work together. Typically, the presenter will set up the build by saying something like 'Moving to a different subject…', they will then look at the screen, the audience watching them, will do the same. Then they will CLICK and watch the slide build making comments. This idea plays an important part throughout our methods as it requires the slide to be designed correctly and the presenter to present correctly, but the power of the technique is beyond doubt and well worth mastering. While we will mention directed attention in several areas of this book, here we are going to look at several visual devices that enable or *require* this technique…

Diagrams

Lozenge

The centre of the lozenge represents the main heading and the segments surrounding it are the subheadings. These are useful for 'Central Ideas' or showing dependencies.

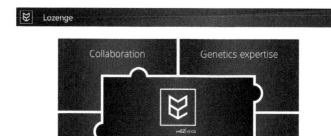

Typically, this will build with the central idea first (although sometimes last – it depends on the patter) and then the other section from the top centre, and clockwise a CLICK at a time, allowing the presenter to add value to each section. It should never be built all at once; there is too much information in it. See:

www.vincis62.com/book/lozenge.html

Schematic

The schematic is very common in presentations, especially technical ones. This schematic from IBM shows how their archiving solution works. The build on these slides is critical, to draw the audience into the explanation of the diagram.

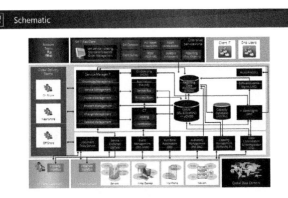

These diagrams need to be built logically following the way the presenter will explain them. Once again, this can be viewed at: www.vincis62.com/book/schematic.html

Pyramid

This example uses a pyramid, showing a tiered structure of supporting ideas.

It is particularly useful when describing anything to do with market segmentation – most markets can be described as a triangle with the smaller clients (of which there are many) at the foot and the higher value or larger clients (of which there are few) at the top.

This slide would be built from bottom to top probably on three CLICKs. View this at:

www.vincis62.com/book/pyramid.html

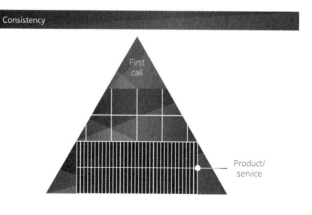

Consistency

First
call

Who are we?

What do we do?

Why engage?

Consistency

First
call

Why need?

Why us?

Divisions or LOB?

Consistency

First
call

Product/
service

Venn

Venn diagrams are very useful. Here we are displaying three areas of a client's competitive advantage and how they overlap to increase customer satisfaction.

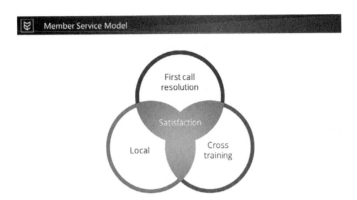

Usually this would build on three CLICKs. To see how this builds, look at: www.vincis62.com/book/venn.html

Matrix

2 × 2 × 2

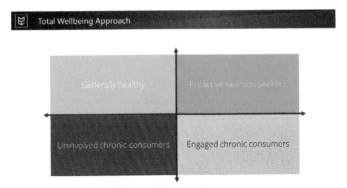

The diagram depicts the changing face of the client's marketplace. In the late 1990s IT was tactical, quantitative, and relatively simple, but recently it has become strategic, more qualitative, and far more complex. The diagram supports the patter.

The build on these matrices is similar to graphs (build axes, then data). To see it presented please use this link: www.vincis62.com/book/2×2×2.html

Basic Techniques

Build Up

The concept of 'pacing information flow' has led us to use a number of graphical techniques. The two most important of these are summarised in the phrase, 'build up, fade down'.

Build up is the idea that a diagram is often too complex to show all at once. As an example, look at the following diagram.

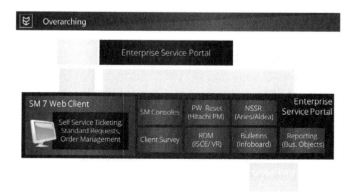

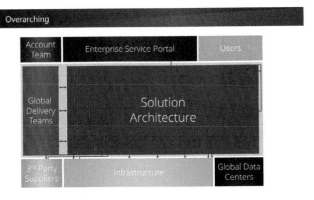

This is a schematic. These diagrams are mostly too complicated for us to want to use in full, so we instead use a simplified version, and take each isolated area individually, exposing the detail there.

This sequence can be seen presented at:

www.vincis62.com/book/ buildup.html

By building the diagram up we show the audience where to look on the slide, thereby ensuring information transfer. We also control the pace of the information flow.

Fade Down

A related, but different, way of simplifying complicated diagrams, is the 'fade down.'

Instead of beginning with small pieces and building them up together, sometimes it is easier to do the opposite, and begin with a complicated image that can then be examined and explained piece-by-piece.

Care must be taken that the initial visual doesn't cause information overload, but in the example shown, this is unlikely.

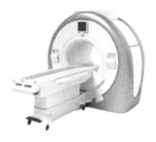

This sequence can be seen presented at:
www.vincis62.com/book/ fade.html

Highlight

This is another useful technique that is easier to recreate in PowerPoint™. For example, here you can see a map and then an area highlighted.

Often we will combine the three techniques, first building up a complex diagram, then fading down all but the relevant piece, and highlighting it at the same time.

Full Map with Highlights

You can view the presentation at:
www.vincis62.com/book/ highlight.html

Zoom-in

Finally, the zoom-in technique, which is particularly useful for spreadsheets, maps and photographs.

Once again, these slides can be seen presented at:
www.vincis62.com/book/zoom.html

Value Proposition Visualisation

A final point: when a Value Proposition slide is actually used and shown, it is best if the five points are presented one at a time. Thus one point is made and shown at a time, and the overall picture builds up and grows in power as it does so.

To reinforce what is an important part of the overall approach, here is a storyboard example.

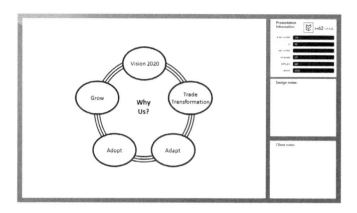

So far, so good. What we now have is a basis for the core of the sales message and also for what we have referred to as the winning slide. But how is this sort of information presented on the slide, and just how is it used? The next section adds some thoughts about the picture that is building, and how to make the overall presentation persuasive and powerful.

Chapter 6

DESIGN

It is only shallow people who do not judge by appearances.
Oscar Wilde

Before I start this chapter a word of caution, I am not a designer. What you are about to read needs to be put into context. The design of the PowerPoint™ slide is important, but not as important as the *purpose* of the slide or the content.

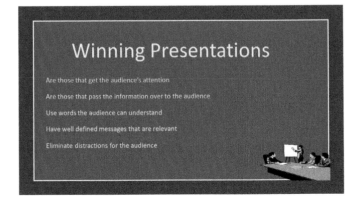

When I present this to a new audience I always point to the graphic in the right hand corner and ask 'What is this?' The correct answer is 'rubbish', however, I usually get 'clip art' as a response.

Then I ask them to do something: next time you see a piece of clip art in a presentation, find the person who put it there originally (because chances are it was not the current user!), and ask them this question, 'Why did you do it?'

The interesting thing about this question is that it doesn't matter where in the world they are, or in what language they speak, the answer is broadly the same: 'Well, it's a dull boring slide, so I thought I would give it some visual interest!'

Half points. This *is* a dull boring slide, however, why do people insist on adding graphics to make up for it? Here is a version designed by Alison Sleightholm, (probably the finest PowerPoint™ designer on the planet). Is it any better?

Winning Presentations
Are those that get the audience's attention
Are those that pass the information over to the audience
Use words the audience can understand
Have well defined messages that are relevant
Eliminate distractions for the audience

A lot of people would think so. Indeed, as a piece of design it is better, nicer to look at, easier to read and the imagery 'keys' the content (see later). But ask yourself this important question, 'Does this new slide improve the information transmission?' Answer: NO.

So why do we do it?

The answer, I believe, lies in the fact that, as presenters, we have been audience members. We know what a heading and five (or six in this case) bullet points feels like. We all know that, regardless of the quality of the graphics, this dull and boring slide is going to need a presenter of rare gift if it isn't going to send us to sleep. So we add a little Clip Art to do nothing else but appease our conscience a little for what we are about to do: *abuse the audience*. Spending time worrying about background images when we could spend time worrying about content is a crime – don't bother.

Drawable Graphics

Let us return to the example of our IT client from earlier. Instead of displaying the Value Proposition as a list we use five bubbles like this:

The first point builds automatically, but the others require individual CLICKs. Not only is this more engaging for the audience, but when you ask the audience to recall the five points, an amazing number of them draw the bubbles first and then label the points. Giving the points a visual layout helps people remember them.

Look at the next slide – this is a typical PowerPoint™ slide, even down to the colours: self-explanatory, and often presented by reading.

At the risk of again repeating myself, this slide will encourage the audience to disengage. Look carefully at the slide and read the text. Clearly, you need to be a cardiologist to understand the content, but you do not need to be a cardiologist to 'see' the picture hiding in the text, can you see it?

We find that about 1 in 50 people can 'see' the picture that supports this patter. The clue is the timeline: note that four of the bullets have a date. The slide is of course talking about the development of something over a period of 50 years and what would be more interesting and engaging would be the sequence shown below.

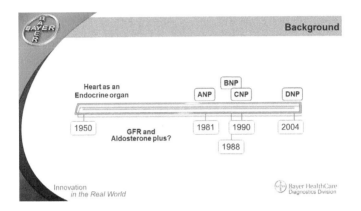

What you can see here is a sequence (one slide but four CLICKs) that builds up as the presenter reads the bullet points of the previous slide. Try it. Or if you prefer, use the following link to see me present them.

www.vincis62.com/book/timeline.html

This slide is not there primarily to act as a cue to the presenter, so ill-prepared that they must read out every word. In any case, very few people can either write the kind of material that reads well when read out, or read well in that kind of way (actors are rightly paid large sums of money to create audio books, for instance, because it demands a real skill). More evidence that very few people can naturally read well is provided by something we see practically every day, the effect that teleprompters have on our politicians. Many read their speeches (no doubt written by someone else, which cannot be helped), but the only punctuation they use is to pause where each line ends; and, because of the physical nature of the teleprompter, the lines themselves are very short. So, what you hear sounds rather like the following looks:

> *Good morning ladies and,*
> *gentlemen I am so very pleased to,*
> *be here in your beautiful city and have the,*
> *opportunity to speak to you about my*
> *congenital punctuation blindness.*

Remember that an audience can read the words on a slide considerably faster than a presenter can read them out loud. Most presentations sound infinitely better if the speaker is well-prepared, and interpreting the brief notes in front of them in light of that preparation – speaking fluently from an outline, rather than reading a full text. If you reduce the words to a list of headings then what remains will certainly be much more manageable (though granted you may need to add in some notes for yourself, to act as the cue that is otherwise now missing).

The Purpose of Design

It may sound as though I don't value design. I do. I think it can make a massive impact on audiences on an emotional level and a smaller impact on a rational level. Slides need to look good, primarily because they are a showcase for your organisation.

Another thing that has always puzzled me is the lack of design in corporate presentations. Can there be a major organisation on the face of the planet that does not put a massive amount of time, effort and often money into getting the corporate communications right? Brochures, web sites, stationery, all designed by a designer, carefully co-ordinated so as to maximise Consistent Integrated Marketing Communications. Then the salesperson gets up with a presentation they pulled together on the flight!

What I find bizarre about many of these organisations is that they will spend fortunes on the literature which is designed to initiate dialogue with a prospect, but then refuse to spend money on the piece of communication that could make that prospect a client. When was the last time you heard a client say 'I gave you the business because your brochure was exceptional?'

On the other hand, a good sales presentation often makes the difference on an order.

So I begin this section on PowerPoint™ design by saying this: don't do it yourself, hire an expert. It's too important to leave to amateur designers such as myself or your PA.

The rest of this section is therefore really aimed at professional designers who have to create presentations for other people to present, although some of the ideas are pretty essential for the actual presenter to understand.

The Communication Problem: Perception

One man's ceiling is another man's floor.

Paul Simon

Look at this picture, 'My wife and my mother-in-law', published in 1915 by W.E. Hill. I am sure you have seen this before; it is very famous. What do you see? Old hag or beautiful woman? Perhaps both or nothing? The really interesting question is what did the person next to you see and how do you know it was the same?

This is the problem with communication: people's perception is subjective. What one person sees as an advantage, others see as a problem. The trick with really good presentations is to minimise the opportunity for misinterpretations and that takes considerable effort. We are once again touching on De Burgh and Steward's concept of *Actual vs. Intended Messages*. I have seen many slides that inadvertently convey a different meaning from the intended, not always positive; here is an example:

This, one of the few slides created solely for this book, is actual data from a presentation given to us on behalf of a client but it was not designed and not used; here is why.

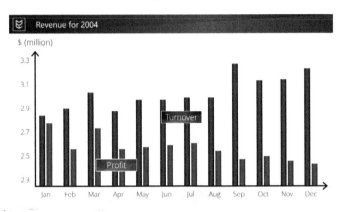

The presenter wants to prove credibility by showing that his company's revenue is growing (a common misconception that size in business matters!). However, I look at this graph and see a company that is trading profit for sales and will shortly run out of cash: not so credible! But I am a sceptic. Again this is a reference to Tim Steward and Hugo De Burgh's concept of Intended and Actual messages. The question we have to ask is 'Can this data be interpreted in a different way?' If so how do we prevent it? The answer here was to remove the profit line – now it just shows a growing company!

Integrated Marketing Communications and Branding

This is not the place for a lengthy discussion about the necessity of having a consistent look and feel for your presentations, or for your entire marketing communications. Other people have written about that topic at length already. However I want to point out that the presentation is a highly visible piece of communication that for some reason tends to get left out of the branding guidelines. It is probably seen by more people for longer than any other piece of marketing collateral and so ought to be at the top of the list when considering branding.

We put considerable effort into promoting consistency with our clients and will often modify the design of a presentation to make it fit with a consistent approach to communication even if they do not have a policy. To this end we almost always produce a corporate ID presentation that helps promote this consistency, both in my team and in the client's presenters. I highly recommend that you produce one for your own organisation.

Look and Feel

I learnt very early on that design is a personal thing.

Having produced over 10,000 PowerPoint™ presentations and, therefore, seen well over 20,000 backgrounds all with different layouts, colours, images, etc. I can say with some clarity that it doesn't really matter. Some people will love it, others will not. The important thing is that it is unique to you and it has been designed by a designer and not put together on the plane.

Good backgrounds have some things in common: contrast, good usable space, and visible but not over-facing branding. Whilst most of these are self-explanatory let me touch on the first one and explain it.

Contrast

The human eye cannot see brightness.

For example, if you were to look at a torch at night and a different torch in the day, could you determine which was the brighter? Probably not. What the human eye can do is compare brightness levels, this is of course called contrast.

Take the two torches and put them side by side in a dark room and you can tell which is brighter. The same goes for computer projection devices; side-by-side you can see a difference but isolated and in different ambient light conditions you can't.

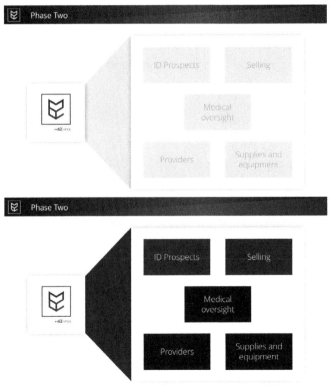

There is a myth about projectors that says brighter is better, but as you actually need a massive increase in light output to see any perceived increase in brightness levels, I am not convinced of its worth. If your image is washed out, it may be considerably cheaper and quicker to control the ambient light than to change the projector for a more expensive, brighter version. I am not advocating that we all sit in the dark to watch presentations (although this can help you sleep if the presenter is using bullet points!), but turning off the fluorescent lights in favour of bright down lighters can have a dramatic effect on contrast levels.

The human eye is a contrast meter, hence find a dark wall to project on to and avoid bright lights sending rays onto the screen.

As far as the look and feel goes, the bigger the contrast between the background and the foreground colours, the easier it is to see. So dark blue backgrounds and bright yellow text can be seen clearly because of the relevant contrast differences. Not that we are advocating using blue and yellow, it's just that you don't put yellow text over a yellow background and then wonder why people can't see the text.

PowerPoint™ Templates

PowerPoint™ templates provide all presentation material with a consistent look and feel. A considerable amount of effort goes into the design of these templates and once complete there are no restrictions on their use within the client organisation.

This is a PowerPoint™ tool that carries some, but not all, of the information to brand a presentation. Each template should be programmed with the following information:

- Main background
- Title screen background
- Default font
- Default colour scheme
- Default animation scheme

Corporate ID Presentation

What is an ID?

A Presentation ID kit consists of a series of template slides reflecting the client's identity. It is useful when you need to speed up the process of slide production, improve quality and consistency and therefore reduce the amount of time and effort required to produce a professional-looking presentation. The purpose of the ID kit is to extend the usefulness of the PowerPoint™ template and to allow users access to additional pieces of design that help them produce visual slides instead of a presentation that is essentially a 'list of lists' using headings and bullet points.

Why do our Clients use them?

Some presentations need to be put together immediately, or additional slides may be added. It is important that these slides do not stand out from the rest by being of poor quality or inconsistent. To this end our clients find the ID kit an invaluable tool. It ensures:

- Quality
- Design Consistency
- Corporate regulation adherence

and reduces the:

- time
- effort
- cost

What is Contained in an ID?

A sample ID presentation can be found by following this link at: www.vincis62.com/book/ID.zip

Broadly the file contains the following items.

PowerPoint™ Template (.pot)

A fully designed and configured template file for use with all the latest versions of PowerPoint™.

Main Background

This is simple, coloured backdrop that we use to enhance legibility and reduce any distractions from the message.

Segue Slides

As well as giving a presentation structure, this helps the audience organise the information and encourages 're-tuning' after they start to 'sample', thus improving the amount of information received and therefore retained from your presentation. It is important that the segue slides have a different background from the rest of the slides..

Heading Banner

Slide titles ought to be visually different from the main body of a slide and, as such, most presentations require the addition of a heading banner to lie behind the title on certain slides.

We always use a contrast colour, so that the title bar isn't confused with a main body element. We add an animated 'wipe' on the title bar to draw the eye, and then fade in the text. If a title repeats from one slide to another, we don't include any animation, because the audience don't need to be alerted to a change.

Effective communication not just impressive presentation

Successful presentations should not only be consistent in content (messaging), but also in style. Slides should be designed so that the imagery directly reflects and links to the message being communicated. This way the audience finds it easy to see how points are interlinked with the general message. For example, using a map of Europe on a slide when you are discussing your company's performance in the European market will reinforce the point and add clarity. We call this 'keying' the slide; the graphic helps the audience place the information in context.

Visually keying information is important in presentations for the same reason; we would typically 'key' the slide with relevant photography (pictures of cranes for a crane hire company, PCs for an IT company, etc.).

The Art of Animation

The ability to simplify means to eliminate the unnecessary so that the necessary may speak.

Hans Hofmann

Purpose of Animating Slides

The purpose of animating a slide is to control the flow of information. Good animation directs the audience's attention to *where* it is required *when* it is required.

Bad animation is distracting.

Done well, animation can add considerable non-verbal information to the overall communication. Done badly, it can ruin a good slide and, therefore, a good presentation.

Animation is integral to the visualisation, the design, the delivery, and almost all of the other sections in this book; it is a core skill.

Build Types

There are two basic types of animation (build) effects: those that leave the object where it is in relation to the slide (*static builds*) and those that move the object in relation to the slide (*motion builds*). Generally, it is the latter that grab more attention, usually too much, and therefore, they are frequently distracting. In general, we only use static builds and motion paths (movements of objects from one place to another). Other builds involving motion tend to do more harm than good. Static builds, on the other hand, are very useful: the most frequently used static build is the *fade*, but I have listed the effects that fall into each category below.

Static Builds

Basic	Dissolve In	Wheel	
Appear	Flash Once	Wipe	**Moderate**
Blinds	Plus		Colour
Box	Random Bars	**Subtle**	Typewriter
Checkerboard	Split	Expand	Unfold
Circle	Stripes	Fade	Zoom
Diamond	Wedge	Faded Swivel	

Motion Builds

We use movement to reflect changes on the slide. Make sure to avoid all repeating movements in animation, as they are very distracting, and only use animation to demonstrate a change to the audience.

Build Times

The principal aim of animating is to draw the audience's attention to the correct place on the screen at the right time. It is not to impress them with how well we know PowerPoint™. We encourage use of simple, non-distracting animation. Perhaps, the reason that presenters use various animation types is that they know their content is so bad they hope some variation in the build types will add something! Good animation should be unnoticed by the audience who should be engaged by the message, not the medium. To this end, consistency is a prerequisite for quality animation.

Build Time is the time it takes between a CLICK and the moment the animation ceases. We tend not to have continuous animation (except on a title slide where we want to draw attention to the slide and will not be presenting over it) as this can be too compelling and audiences have difficulty paying attention to the presenter if things are moving. Because of this, we recommend that build times do not exceed three seconds. As we also recommend that presenters say nothing over slide builds, to allow the audience to concentrate on assimilating the information just displayed, three seconds is a comfortable amount of silence. Silences much longer than that require a great deal of self-control from the presenter, which is difficult with raised adrenalin levels.

Arrows

Flying arrows don't work. Generally, arrows should be 'wiped' in the direction of their indication as this naturally draws the eye towards what they are pointing to.

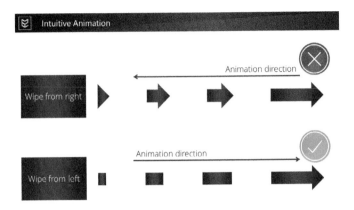

Clearly this is difficult to do in 2D – you can see a more detailed demonstration of how to do this by following this link: www.vincis62.com/book/intiativeanimation.html

Wheels

Wheels, like the lozenge, can be useful in demonstrating the relationship between headings.
www.vincis62.com/book/winningslide.html

Flow Charts

There are two types of flow charts, linear and iterative (see the visualisation section for explanation). They need to animate from the start of the process to the end.

To see this presented use this link:

www.vincis62.com/book/flowchart.html

Graphs

Axes are usually built using a static build, but data is usually *wiped* again in the intuitive direction. So bar graphs are *wiped from bottom*, line graphs *wiped from left*, etc. Comparators are usually *wiped in in the direction of increase/decrease* – again these are more easily demonstrated online:

www.vincis62.com/book/graphs.html

2D Model

2D modelling can be useful to show a cross-section or schematic view of a complex object, especially where attention needs to be directed towards one very specific aspect of its construction and it is important to avoid distraction by unnecessary modelling. See:

www.vincis62.com/book/ 2d.html

3D Model

The use of 3D models can be invaluable to convey understanding, especially for technical subjects. Here we have built a 3D image in Photoshop™ to show a picture of something that has yet to be constructed. See:

www.vincis62.com/book/3d.html

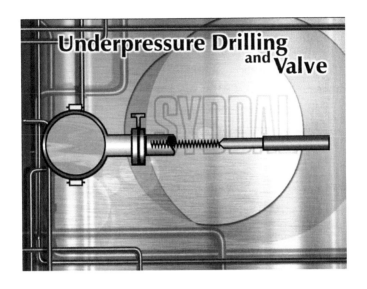

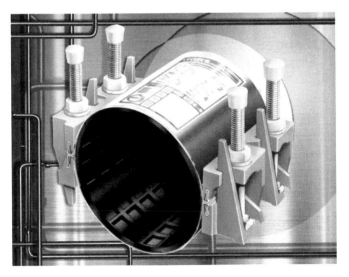

4D Model

By a 4D model we mean a 3D model that is built over time; here is the previous example shown in the stages of assembly. View at: www.vincis62.com/book/4dmodel.html

Repeated Slides

The first time a slide appears in a presentation it should build, but if it appears again the repeated build will just irritate the audience. We, therefore, recommend that the whole slide just builds at once (unless the title changes, in which case I prefer to build the title bar, then the title and then build the rest of the slide).

Again this is demonstrated online:
www.vincis62.com/book/repeats.html

Repeated Objects

In the same vein, objects that are repeated on adjacent slides and do not move (see later) should not disappear only to reappear immediately after in the same place.

Examples of this can be seen online:
www.vincis62.com/book/repeatedobjects.html

Subjective *vs.* Objective Quality

One man's Picasso is another man's art!

NT

There are two definitions of quality, which may be termed 'objective' and 'subjective'. Subjective quality is a bit like art; whether you like it or not depends largely on the individual. Look through some of the examples in this book of slides we have designed: some of them you will like and some of them you will not. People have favourite colours, prefer some shapes over others etc.

If a presentation we have produced fails a subjective quality test, we don't worry too much, we just redo it for the client. We try to ensure that these matters of taste are decided early on, but generally we will not be hard on the designers if somebody doesn't like the design.

Objective quality is another issue. On these things they are either right or wrong – it is *not* down to taste. Spelling, conformity to the brief, the way things animate, and the way things are lined up all form part of our Objective Quality Standards, and it is against this list that our quality audit process runs.

The list of Objective Quality Standards (OQS) overleaf may help you with your presentations; they certainly help in producing ours.

Chapter 7

OBJECTIVE QUALITY STANDARDS

Quality is not an act, it's a habit.

Aristotle

OQS Guiding Principles

Our Objective Quality Standards are designed to help us make the most effective presentations. They're based on a combination of psychological research and our years of experience. Broadly, the principles of OQS fall into one of a few categories:

Use a Visual Language

Communicating visually is usually more efficient and less ambiguous than with text alone. In addition, research suggests that textual communication works separately to communication with images, meaning that 'dual coding' can occur when both are used together (Paivio, 1971). To do this efficiently, it is necessary to establish a clear, consistent and relevant visual language. Several of our rules seek to help do this, so that we can maximise use of graphics but so the audience always knows what each graphic means.

Reduce Distraction

Research suggests that there is a strong link between problem-solving and learning, and that mental resources (cognitive load) directed towards one are unavailable for the other (Sweller, 1988).

This is at the core of our OQS – reducing cognitive load spent on anything other than those things we want to audience to recall.

To this end, we seek to remove distractions whenever possible. We also aim to present information to the audience in the most digestible format so that they require the minimum cognitive load to unpick a message (leaving the maximum available for memorising it).

Direct Attention

In addition to reducing distractions, we also seek to positively direct the audience's attention. By encouraging them to focus on those things that we want them to see and remember, we boost recall of the important messaging points.

Following on from Cognitive Load theory, it has been demonstrated that when information is presented in different media at the same time, people struggle to comprehend multiple strands of information at once. This is known as the 'split attention effect.' If the presenter is talking at the same time as something is happening on the screen, and if they aren't directly complimentary, the audience will often be forced to choose which to pay attention to. This sacrifices the presenter's control over the audience's attention.

Eliminate Unintentional Meaning

There are many ways to convey meaning in a Presentation.

It's beneficial to make use of as many media of information exchange as possible. This means making sure that we don't convey information inadvertently, and instead always convey information as we mean it.

There are many examples of inadvertent meaning, but two of the most important causes, for our purposes, are spatial and temporal contiguity. (Moreno and Mayer, 1999). This is the idea that simply displaying two objects or concepts close together in space or time can imply a relationship between them. This can be used to create a connection between two concepts, which can be useful. However, if no connection is intended (or if a connection between equally similar items could be distorted), we must be careful not to imply one.

Communicate Effectively

Often it is possible to allow design principles to get in the way of effective communication. Our OQS lays out a set of rules on text and slide backgrounds that prevents the audience from being able to unable to read slides or interpret graphics on them.

Wherever possible, we have aimed to give an example of each OQS rule on paper. For obvious reasons, particularly for those rules regarding animation, this was sometimes very difficult, so all rules have a complete, animated example at:
www.vincis62.com/book/oqs

Overarching

Everything on the slide should have a purpose – If an animation, click, or object is being included, it must add something towards our goal.

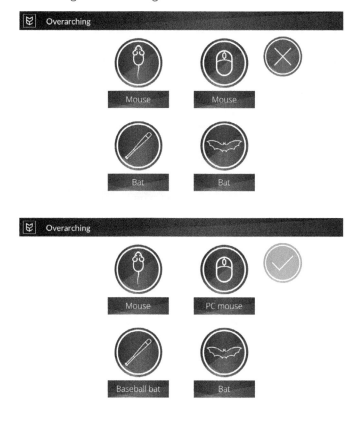

Direct attention using animation and build – lead the audience's attention to where you want it to be. Don't include any elements that might distract the audience's attention.

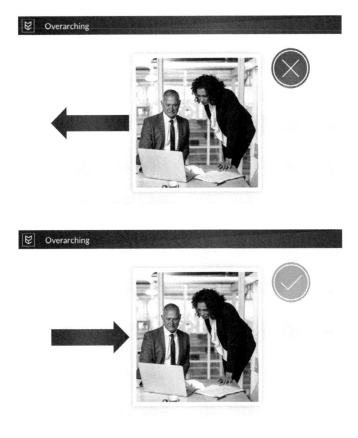

There should be no ambiguity of meaning – It's important that the audience can reasonably interpret only the meaning we want them to from a slide. Any ambiguity should be resolved.

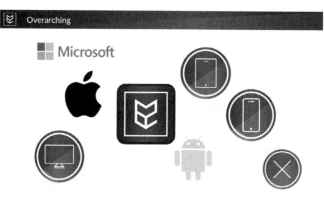

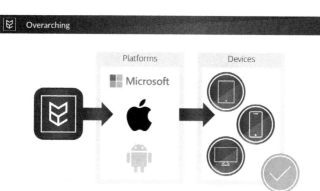

Simplified Complexity – Choose the simplest way to do things. Unnecessary complexity is confusing.

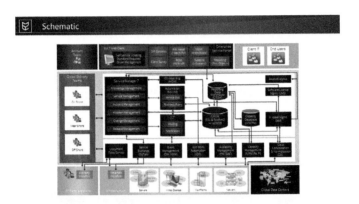

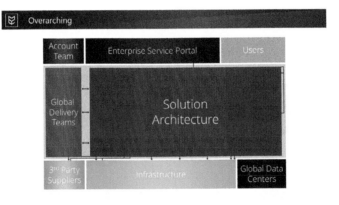

PowerPoint™ Template

Title slides should have a visibly different background to the rest of the presentation – This offers some visual demarcation to the structure.

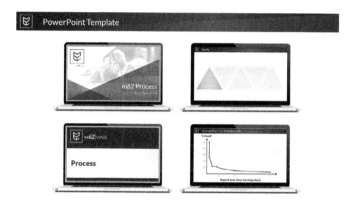

The title bar must contrast with the main slide background – When the title changes, the audience's eyes need to be drawn to new title. The titles, therefore, must offer a contrast with the main body.

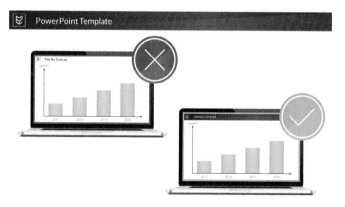

The title bar should always be in the same place on each slide – Otherwise the audience doesn't know immediately where to look for the title bar.

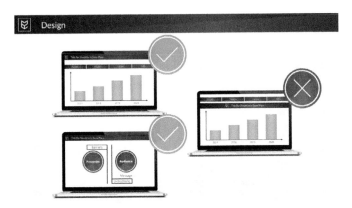

The title bar needs to animate in a way, which draws the audience's eye to follow it to its final position – When the title changes, it's important that the audience notices, and pays attention to this.

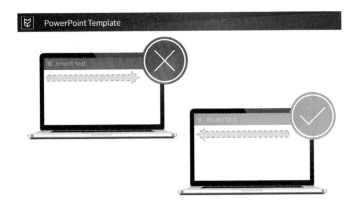

Visual Cognitive Dissonance

Points of Dissonance should always be resolved – The benefit of VCD is that it captures the audience's attention. This allows higher recall when used properly, but has the capacity to work as a very powerful distraction if it doesn't resolve.

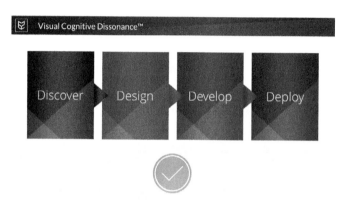

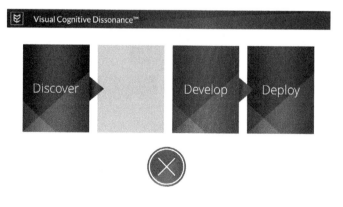

Slide position should not convey unintended meaning –

Unintended VCD (created by positioning in the slide etc.) is as distracting as properly used VCD is attention-grabbing.

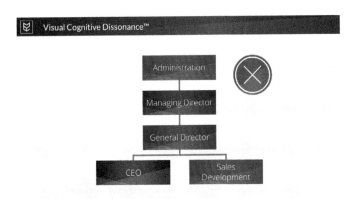

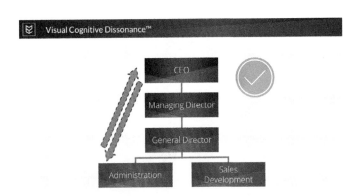

Design

Never distort a PowerPoint object or image – All images should be proportional. Squashed or stretched images look unprofessional and can be more difficult to interpret.

Objects that are similar need to have similar graphical treatments.

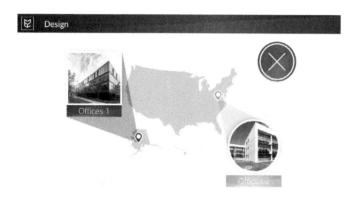

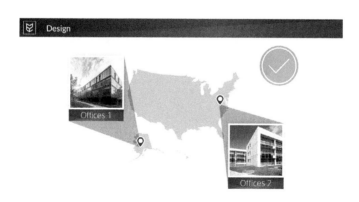

Objects that are different need to be graphically different.

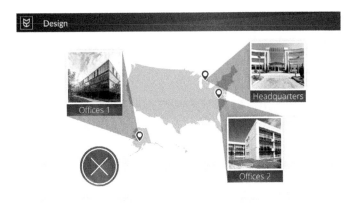

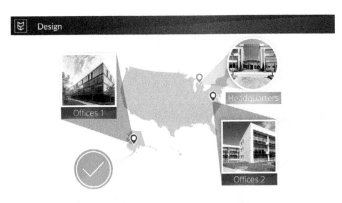

This ensures that the design language is properly reflective of the meaning (so that it doesn't accidentally convey similarity or difference when it isn't implied).

Where possible use logos rather than text – Logos often contain less ambiguity than text and are quicker to interpret.

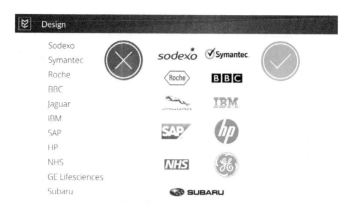

Text must have enough space within its holder – Cramped text is more difficult to read.

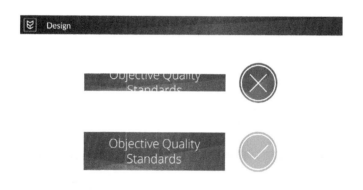

Value Proposition

A 'Value Proposition' graphic should only be used on 'Value Proposition' slides – It should not appear on general content slides. The Value Proposition should be distinct to the audience to the rest of the presentation.

Using the same graphic for something other that the 'Value Proposition' lessens its impact and loses credibility by hindering communication and confusing the message. The graphic must be exclusive to the 'Value Proposition' slide.

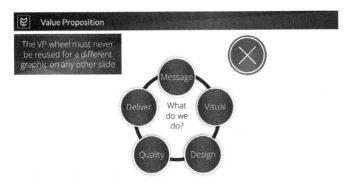

The Value Proposition must animate in with a separate click for each benefit – This creates Visual Cognitive Dissonance, gives the presenter control over information pacing, and allows the Value Proposition to build up slowly.

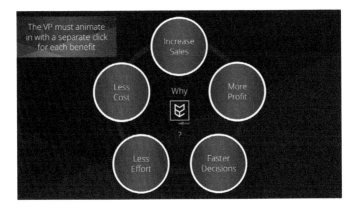

Subsequent Value Proposition graphics should highlight in a contrasting colour specifically to show where in the presentation the presenter is – This presents the audience from becoming briefly lost, which distracts them. It is also quicker than a full build-up, but still has a similar effect.

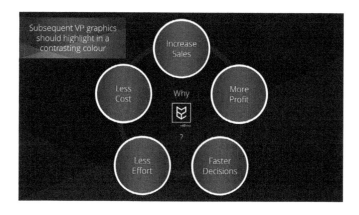

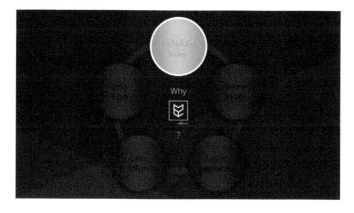

The background of a VP should always contrast the rest of the presentation – signals to the presenter and to the audience the difference between the Value Proposition and the proof points.

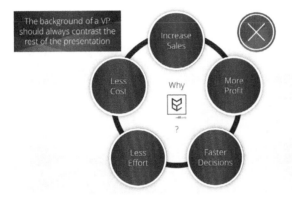

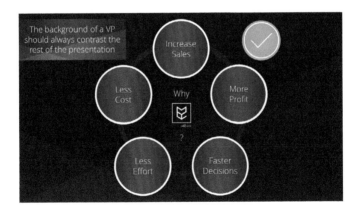

Graphs, Charts and Tables

Graphs should always automatically animate in axis (and text) first, followed by each data set (not point) on a click

Animation is essential in presenting a graph slide by allowing the presenter to guide the audience and enabling them to understand what is essentially a complicated slide.

By animating the graph in this way, you are allowing the presenter to control the pace of information and explain to the audience what they are seeing, before revealing the next set of data, in order to assist in the assimilation of data.

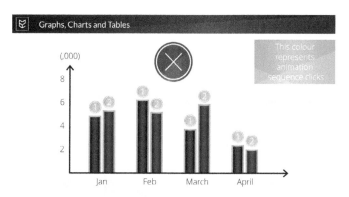

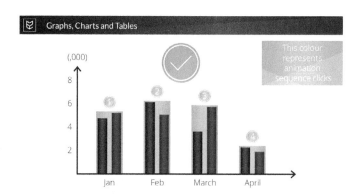

Always use labels instead of legends – It is difficult for an audience to make the association between a legend, which is placed independently of a graph, and the corresponding data sets.

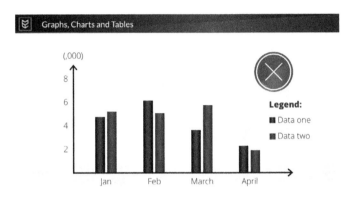

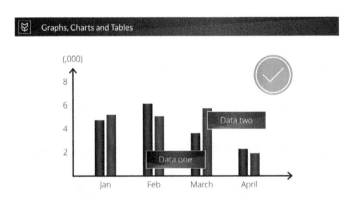

The header rows of a table should always be shaded differently to the main body of the table – Different shading for the header rows of tables makes them visually different, which makes them easier to read. Likewise, sometimes the first column (for example, if it contains names or titles) should also be shaded differently.

Photos

Photos of people looking out of the screen should be avoided – When someone looks you in the eye, your attention is diverted to their eyeline. The same happens in presentations, meaning an audience may miss the other information that is crucial to the message.

Have people in photograph's direct gaze into the slide and/or at object of interest – The attention of the audience will naturally follow whatever people in the photo are looking at.

Iconography should be: repeated, common or not used – An icon that is associated with a particular word/ meaning on one slide should be used consistently for that word/meaning throughout the presentation. Use of a common icon allows recognition by the audience. This is lost if the icons are inconsistent.

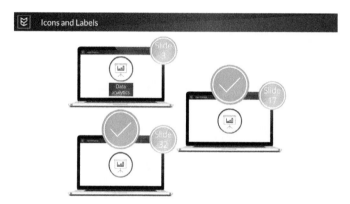

The 1st time a symbol or icon is shown it should be labeled with text (including photos and design elements)
– This removes ambiguity

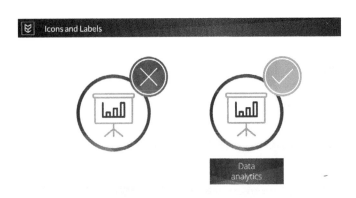

After an icon has been labelled, it does not need to be labelled again – Reduces unnecessary text, which can serve as a distraction

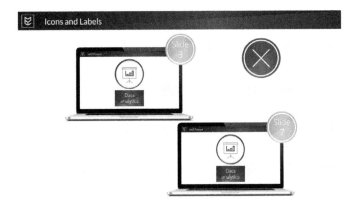

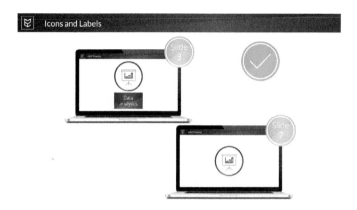

Label 1 icon at a time – This directs the audience's attention and allows the presenter to dictate pacing of information flow.

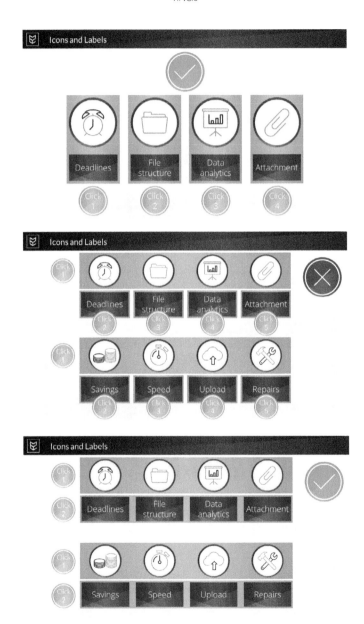

Text

Text should always have a strong contrast to the background onto which it is placed – Subtle colour differences between text and background result in the content being illegible to the audience. Some projectors considerably lower the contrast ratio viewed and, therefore, an almost exaggerated contrast ratio is necessary.

Minimum text size should be 24 points – Text must be legible. Considerable research and experience has shown that a text size smaller than 24 points is likely to be illegible to an audience member sitting at the rear of the room or auditorium.

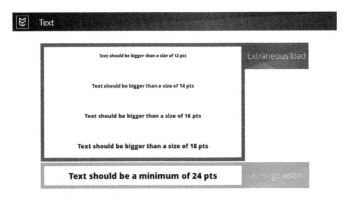

Text should never be displayed on the vertical. Whether that is by rotating a text box by 90° or by formatting the text to run top to bottom, rather than left to right – By using text format in this way, the presenter runs the risk of disengaging the audience as they attempt to decipher what is written. Audiences have been observed tilting heads in order to interpret text displayed vertically.

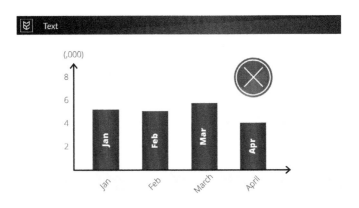

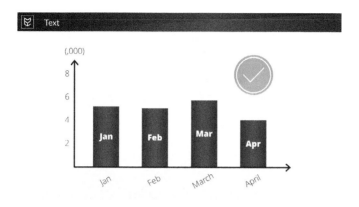

Text case should always be consistent – As a general rule, text case for titles and sentence case for main body text is by far the most effective method. Don't use a combination of the two in any other way. Otherwise the change in text case can look slightly odd, distracting the audience.

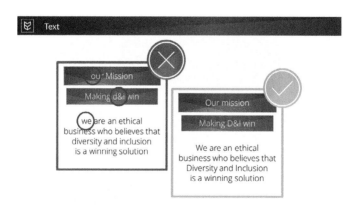

Do not squash paragraph spacing on text boxes excessively — Excessive paragraph formatting in a text box can distort the text once the presentation is in 'show mode.' This can make the text difficult to read.

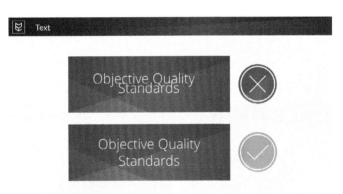

m62 default setting for line spacing is 1.0

Scripted fonts should be avoided in favour of an MS sans serif font – This font type is very difficult to read.

Animation

Animation order should not covey unintended sequence – All elements must animate in a way that makes sense or you confuse the message

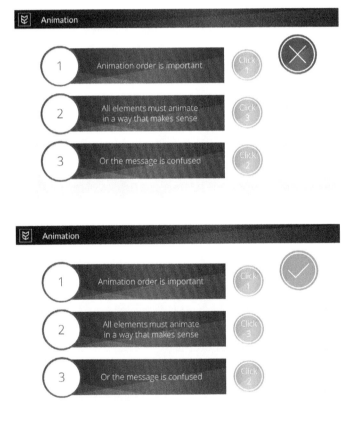

If an existing element changes, it should always morph from its previous position to its new location (motion paths).

If an object needs to move from an existing position to a new position it should motion path rather than animating out and back in again.

If the graphic has already been displayed on a previous slide, only to appear on the following slide, but its location needs to change, it should remain in the same place (without animating in again), then animate to its new location.

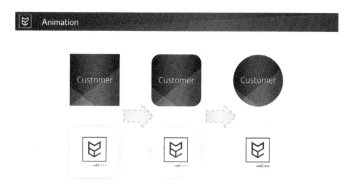

Slide content animated in this way engages the audience's attention and helps them easily understand the flow of information being presented. If the graphic exits and then reappears, the audience can become confused into thinking that they are looking at a different piece of information to that which was previously seen.

Use visually associated animation – Animation should be logical (e.g. if you have an arrow pointing right, have it wipe in from left to right). Visually associated animation directs the audience's attention to *where* it is required.

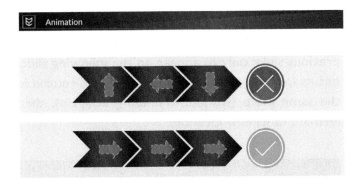

Never animate anything that has already appeared on a previous slide – Once the slide has been built up once, it is more time effective to have the slide open without animation. There is no VCD if people have already seen the complete slide, so reanimation usually serves no purpose, takes too much time, and is boring.

Animation should not take longer than 3 seconds – Long animations cause the presenter to stop what they are saying in order for the slide to catch up. This can leave an uncomfortable silence. This is not to say that the whole slide needs to animate to completion in 3 seconds. Clicks should be used for pauses for the presenter to fill with the narrative flow.

Main body graphics animate in a minimum of 0.5 seconds after titles – Leaving a small delay after the title bar animation enables the audience to read and digest the slide title before delivering the rest of the information.

Never leave an animation repeating until the end of the slide or next click – Continuous motion has been found to draw the eye much more than static images. Therefore the audience will find it difficult to draw their attention away from the slide. This results in the presenter having to compete with the distracting animation. (Matthews, Benjamin and Osborne, 2007)

Animation should be simple – Animation must be kept simple and engaging, enhancing the power of the message. Overly flamboyant animation effects distract the audience.

Only use Motion Animations to convey meaning – Movement is eye-catching and distracting, so should only be used when it is conveying information.

Text should animate in its entirety and not slower than reading pace – Never animate text by letter or by word at a time (in a sentence). Attempts to control the audience's reading speed will irritate them, and serves no real benefit.

Use the title bar to alert the audience that the slide title has changed – With the inclusion of a contrasted bar and a correct use of an animation, the audience are instantly aware that the slide title has changed.

The Process

If we believe, after taking a brief, that the difference between winning and losing a bid will depend in part on the quality of the communication, then we are usually confident enough to adjust our fee accordingly and share the risk with the client. As such we are careful to track the effectiveness of our approach. Each year since inception we have succeeded in helping clients win over 75% of their key specific bids, winning a total of over £3 billion worth of business.

How is this possible?

We have shown the following example hundreds of times at seminars and then we show a progressive improvement in layout and design from one to the next. What these slides show is an evolutionary sequence.

1. A very traditional slide presenting a list of points in full. Put up as one unit, it is clear what it means and it can be read more quickly than a presenter can read it aloud, leaving the audience bored and with people's minds wandering until the speaker catches up and moves on.

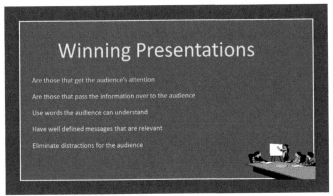

2. The second slide reduces the text and looks better because of it, the audience have less to read, and so may listen to the presenter. But as they still know what is going to be talked about, they may tune out anyway until the next slide is delivered. It is still a list.

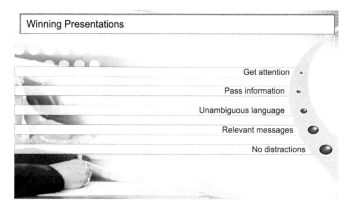

3. The third slide is laid out not as a list but as a Mind Map™ type layout, with the central idea in the centre of the screen and the bullet points laid out around it. To improve the slide further, it is built up with five CLICKs, preventing the audience members from reading ahead and so forcing them to listen to the presenter. Most people agree that this third version is a significant improvement on the first; however I still don't like it too much. It is still self-explanatory. What is the purpose of the presenter if the audience can discern the information on their own by simply reflecting on the completed slide? There is a better way.

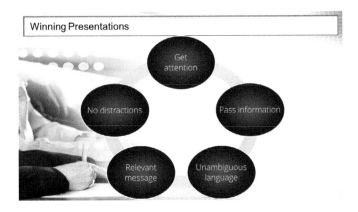

4. I want you to look at the fourth slide. I introduce this to
    the audience as articulating the same information as the
    last three slides but in a visual manner, then I CLICK and
    two balls appear labelled *Presenter* and *Audience*. I pause,
    look at the screen and then look at the audience. They
    all follow my gaze to the screen and then look at me
    expectantly, sometimes with a confused look on their
    faces. The incomplete diagram does not of itself articulate
    my point, they know that *something is missing* and they
    want to know what I have to say over this diagram that
    makes the point. Stop for a minute and examine the last
    sentence *'they want to know what I have to say'*.

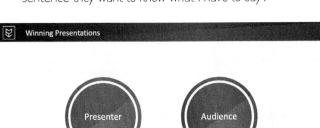

When was the last time you were in a presentation and *actually wanted to listen to the presenter?* More importantly, how much more effective would your presentations be if your audience listened to every single word you said? The audience are at this point utterly engaged in communication with me, I have their rapt attention and usually you can hear a pin drop. I point this out to them and then say 'there are three essential ingredients to an effective presentation', I look at the screen (still two balls) – I have done it again in a different way.

They have just been told there are three things, but they can only see two. This creates *Visual Cognitive Dissonance.* CLICK

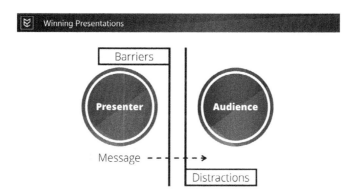

5.   Then I finish the diagram off; I explain that the line in the middle represents barriers to communication and that the third element has to be a message (SMART, see later). The definition of a good presentation is this and only this: 'To what extent do we manage to get the message…' CLICK (message begins to move to the

right) '... across to the audience'. Nothing else matters – they don't have to like it, agree with it or enjoy the experience; they just have to understand the message.

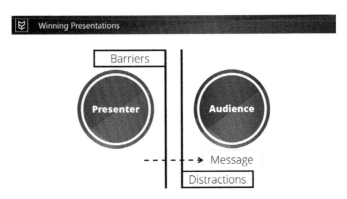

Again this is best seen presented and can be viewed on www.vincis62.com/book/cuecards.html

Chapter 8

TYPES OF
PRESENTATION

If you don't know what you want to achieve, your audience never will.

Harvey Diamond

Four types of presentational intention

In my experience there are essentially four main kinds of presentation, and the difference between them lies, unsurprisingly, in their intention. A presentation can aim to:

- **Persuade:** to get someone to agree with your point of view on a rational level and commit to the action you suggest (buying the product or service in the case of selling, or taking a step towards doing so).

- **Educate:** or inform in a way where the main aim is to impart information; though in transferring a skill there is also a clear link to prompting action.
- **Entertain:** the purpose of the presentation is for the audience to enjoy the experience.
- **Motivate:** to persuade on an emotional level to change (or reinforce) behaviour.

Persuasive Presentations

Management cannot be expected to recognise a good idea unless it is presented to them by a good salesman.

David M Ogilvy

There are many ways of viewing the sales process. People talk of 'consultative selling', 'solution selling', 'interactive and creative selling' (what else?) and refer to patented approaches such as SPIN™. Essentially, the overall approach that all these espouse is logical and depends on a similar view of how people buy. The sales process should certainly not be structured just on the basis of the path of least resistance, doing what's expedient rather than effective.

A good definition of sales (one that reflects customer focus and an understanding of the buyer decision making process) is simply: 'Sales is helping people to buy'.

Each year billions of dollars are invested in training salespeople on sales techniques and relationship building. Everybody knows that you cannot help people to buy until you have uncovered and explored their needs. So salespeople are trained to know how to open and close a sales call, how to ask questions, how to handle objections, when to explore options, the stage of the sales/buyer cycle when you should present solutions, and how to ask for the order.

Organisations know that to achieve their goals it is imperative to have a common sales process in order to manage opportunities more effectively and more efficiently. There are many benefits that are realised by having a common sales process, one being that a sales force has a common language. When a salesperson is selling to me, I can tell very quickly whether they are trained to a particular process. This gives me comfort in knowing that I'm dealing with an organisation that recognises the value of training and developing their salespeople.

However, of all the billions of dollars invested in training, very little, if any of that is invested in the sales *presentation* process. And they're missing a golden opportunity. The difference between winning and losing is a razor's edge – the *competitive* edge. The competitive edge, especially in a 'beauty parade' pitch, is more often than not, the presentation. PowerPoint™ is an incredibly powerful sales tool that can give you that edge. With the correct presentation process you can kill the competition, and not the audience!

A Persuasive Sales Presentation Process

We tend to assume that decisions in the business world are all rational. This is unlikely as there is always an element of the emotional. The decision maker may 'like' the salesperson, have a relationship they value or just dislike something. However, our experience is that rational arguments are far more persuasive than emotional ones and only fail when they are either slim or badly articulated, thus allowing the emotional arguments to prevail.

To this end we tend to assume that the single most important factor in influencing a decision is how well the rational arguments are made. In essence, how well the sales presentation is written, designed and delivered. We do not ignore the relationships that will influence the emotional decisions, nor do we ignore the impact of design and multi-media in manipulating the emotional decisions, but here we will concentrate on how we deliver the rational arguments.

A typical presentation process would look like this:

1. Empathy.
2. Credibility.
3. Benefit.
4. Justification.
5. Close.
6. Questions and answers.

Empathy: people buy from people, especially people with whom they have a connection. That is, you must demonstrate an understanding of the audience to whom you are speaking. This starts in planning – which must originate a tailored presentation, one appropriately directed at the organisation and the people to whom it is being delivered – and is augmented by the presenter's manner and how they handle the initial stages of the presentation.

Whilst, realistically, many people make presentations that are, in fact, similar to numerous others they have made, what matters here is the feeling. If a presentation appears to be too 'standard' – *it's obviously what they say to all their potential clients* – then this is resented, and is likely to be seen as not taking sufficient trouble, or as a sign of insufficient understanding. This can then dilute attention and effectiveness.

Credibility: sell yourself, your company and your product in that order. There is a role here for evidence and proof (including external facts and figures); another element of this is the presenter's, and the presenting company's, credentials. Social proof, case studies, endorsements and testimonials are useful material here, providing independent comment on how your product or service has led to others' success.

They must be expressed succinctly, and positioned early on.

Beware! There is a style of presentation where the need for establishing credentials simply takes over and submerges, or postpones, other detail; or both. One example we witnessed was in a London-based financial company, who will not be named to spare their blushes. For a while every presentation they conducted began with the same 34 slides detailing the history and organisation of the company. These were used, in part, because they were familiar. They were felt to get the presentation and the presenter off to a good start. Their lack of relevance, for certainly the detail was way beyond what was necessary, and the time it took to go through them negated any good effect they may have had.

Indeed, having bored people, they prevented the remainder of the presentations from striking the right note. The initial purchasing decision was made, negatively, long before this part of the presentation was complete.

The Right Tool for the Job

Since 1997 my company has been involved in creating over 3,000 PowerPoint™ presentations for clients. The vast majority of these were sales presentations. These typically fall into two different categories that we call *General* and *Specific*.

General sales presentations are those that are used by a salesforce every day:

• Who are we?
• What do we do?
• Why do clients deal with us?

They are broadly the same and it is possible to design a presentation that allows the salesperson to *spin* (give subtle different meanings to) the presentations to suit most client-facing opportunities. We have clearly demonstrated that a consistent, well thought-out value proposition, well-articulated in a visual PowerPoint™ presentation can increase sales. There is an element of self-selection in the sample set, as people often don't ask for our help unless they are losing. So assuming you close 1 in 3 of your deals, which is we feel average, then you should expect to see an increase to around 3 in 4 by sorting out your general sales presentation.

Specific sales presentations are those that see the light of day once and then are forgotten — regardless of impact or success. After all a dentist would never use someone else's crown in another patient's mouth. These presentations are when the contract value is so large or the client too valuable as to warrant special attention. In these situations no self-respecting salesperson would run the risk of not making the client feel important by writing a presentation about them, what they need and how their problems will be solved. In fact, we have done so many of these that we have developed a process for producing them.

Educational Presentations

Tell me and I'll forget;
Show me and I may remember;
Involve me and I'll understand.

Chinese Proverb

There is a saying that 'those who can, do and those who can't, teach'. It is clearly a saying uttered only by those people who either have never taught or have no idea about how to go about it. I was fortunate at school and had some incredible teachers, particularly for mathematics. As I passed my exams a year early, I had a year at school at the age of 16 when I didn't have any maths lessons to attend. I was asked to help teach some students who were having difficulty. The experience has stayed with me my whole life. The lessons I learnt about teaching mathematics to 12 year olds have helped me teach a huge number of subjects to a huge number of people; from diving to presenting, sales to sailing. Here's the point: there is a process to teaching. If you follow the process you can teach almost anything to anybody.

The process of teaching

My experience is that the process of teaching goes something like this:

- **Credibility:** they have to think you know what you're talking about even if you don't!
- **Motivation:** they have to want to learn.
- **Language:** there has to be an understanding of the language used within the subject matter (e.g. it is difficult to teach a person to sail without using the words 'sheet in' or 'duck!' [duck as in 'lower your head' rather than 'best served with plum sauce']).
- **Basic concepts:** the simple ideas that build to complex ones.
- **Complex ideas:** the ideas underpinning the subject.
- **Understanding:** the pinnacle of success when they understand the subject and can make use of it (possibly even teach it themselves!).

Put simply, you teach by finding out what the audience know already, then breaking down the things they need to know into bite size chunks that they can understand, and then presenting it to them in a language they are familiar with. It sounds simple, but is probably the hardest thing in the world to do well.

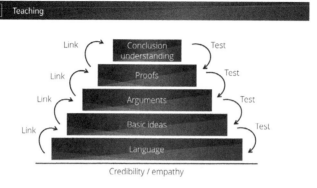

I call this the pyramid of learning; each layer is bigger than the one above it suggesting that in order to teach you have to have good foundations. Each layer is linked (by showing the audience relevance!) and then at each stage the presenter needs to check understanding by asking questions.

Structure

So broadly we would structure a training presentation like this:

- Who are we?
- What are we going to teach?
- Why do you need this?
- Language definition
- Questions and answers
- Basic ideas
- Questions and answers
- Arguments, proofs
- Questions and answers
- Conclusions
- Questions and answers.

Teaching presentations are never the same. Audiences always have different levels of understanding and assimilate information at different speeds. The most important skill for the trainer is to keep people engaged (the right slides clearly help) and this necessitates an element of audience control to maintain the appropriate pace and path of information delivery. Questions asked by the audience will divert the path and may require you to skip through the material in a non-linear fashion.

Audience participation is critical to success in teaching environments. As the Chinese proverb at the head of this chapter says, involvement is the key to understanding. You cannot teach by preaching. Therefore teaching presentations must be flexible and the presenter must be ready to move wherever is required in the material.

Pace

Again, the single biggest mistake in this type of presentation, as with all presentations, is in providing too much information too quickly. Present too little information and interested audiences in an interactive environment will ask for more detail; present too much detail and audiences go to sleep regardless of the environment. The key to success is to pace the information to suit the audience; frequent questioning not only involves them in the process, but it also allows the presenter to gauge the pace: if they are lost then slow down; bored, then speed up.

Questioning

Questioning is an important part of the learning process – both questions asked by the presenter to check or gauge understanding and those asked by the student. They are important partly because of the reasons why the questions are asked and partly because of what they reveal about the inquirer.

Open and closed questions

Amongst many things that are necessary in training people to dive, one must ensure that they truly understand and appreciate Boyle's Law. This is the law that links the volume of a gas to the pressure it is under. Take an inflated balloon under the water, and the deeper it goes the more the increasing pressure of the water compresses it – it gets smaller. Conversely, as it rises towards the surface, with the pressure reducing, the balloon expands.

Why is this important? Imagine you are at a depth of ten metres and you hold your breath and swim to the surface. As the air expands in your lungs (balloons), it has nowhere to go and it can cause serious damage – ultimately bursting a lung or causing an air embolism.

The trick to diving then is not to hold your breath, ever! So that as the air in your lungs expands it can escape and do no damage. Continuous breathing is essential to diving safely but is difficult to do and counter-intuitive since it is instinctive to hold your breath underwater.

Now suppose a student having listened to the above explanation was to ask the following closed question:

'So are you suggesting that if I held my breath at 20 metres and started to ascend quickly I would be dead before I passed the ten metre mark?'

Clearly the answer is 'Yes'. However what is interesting is not the answer but the question. Look at it again, but this time ask yourself 'Does this student think they understand?'

Because they have phrased a closed question you can hear that they are seeking affirmation for something they think they understand; by asking this question they are checking their comprehension.

Now consider the same enquiry but asked as an open question:

'What happens if I surface from 20 metres?'

The probability is that the questioner does not fully understand, they certainly don't think they get it, and more information is necessary. This is almost a cry for help.

Teachers probably do this instinctively. By listening carefully to questions and determining whether they are open or closed we can tell where the student is in their search for comprehension and therefore gauge how effective our teaching is.

This has a profound effect on information flow.

Effect on attention span

Earlier I said attention span is only really about 20 minutes; this tends to be longer in teaching presentations, if the audience has the desire to learn; but it is still not an hour, nor is it all day. The harder the subject matter and the longer the course the shorter these segments need to be. No more than three attention spans without a hard break, and remember that at the end of the day (when they are tired) attention span may drop to ten minutes, and so the last section should be no more than 30 minutes in duration (as opposed to 90 minutes first thing).

The recap

Particularly when teaching, where the objective is to impart knowledge, it is important that after each break (hard or soft) the presenter recaps. This is primarily to ensure understanding but also to help the audience position the information, both in their minds and in the context of the course outline; people like to know what they are doing, why, and what's next.

After a soft break I usually recap the content of the previous attention span and after a hard break the contents of the previous segment. Usually I will ask a question or two to check understanding and to draw the audience back into engagement.

Persuading and educating

Certainly, sometimes both persuading and educating may have to be addressed in the same presentation, but it must always be clear which is occurring. The objectives set the scene: if you intend to prompt someone to agree with you, or buy from you – and thus that they must accept the credibility of what you say, then you are *persuading*. If you simply want them to know something, then you are *educating or informing*.

The two different types of presentation are just that: different – not just in their objectives, but almost everything:

- Pace
- Duration
- Content depth
- Question-handling.

The example we use most to describe the difference is question-handling. As a 'teacher' I must answer students' queries. The implication here is that educational presentations must *answer questions*. But this is *not* the same in selling. In a sales pitch, questions are often best not answered directly, but responded to with another question. Again, more later.

This much alone will begin to focus a presentation in the right kind of way. The process we are touching on here is important. As we are focusing particularly on sales presentations we need to investigate more about exactly what it is in a pitch that can make it successful at persuading and link it to the nature of a winning presentation.

Solution selling

Frequently this provokes objections from people who sell complex or technical products or services. The argument is that in order to sell my product I have to teach the prospect about it. This is possibly the most difficult type of selling, primarily because the salesperson has to fulfil both roles: salesman and teacher (or technician). The best rule of thumb is to distinguish these roles by using both a salesperson and a separate technician or educator. If this is not possible then use two presentations – the education piece and then a separate sales piece; *what is it? –* Teach, *why buy it? –* Sell.

If you must teach and sell at the same time during a presentation then we advise that you use two different backgrounds in the presentation, one for teaching slides and another for sales slides, and coach them to behave differently in each scenario. You will find your sales people more effective if teaching and selling are kept separate if at all possible.

Entertaining Presentations

The purpose of Entertaining Presentations is purely and simply for the audience to enjoy themselves. They might take place at conferences, after dinner or as wedding speeches. Or, if you fancy trying your hand at stand-up comedy, this is the section of the book that you'll be interested in.

First, a word about using comedy in business. Many gurus will advise against it, and often with good reason. However, if you are a confident speaker and out-going personality, with the right guidance you could use comedy to enhance your business presentations without too much difficulty.

In creating Nicci and using my presentation expertise to devise Nicci's stand-up routine, I became interested in how humorous performance could be applied to get across a serious message. Both my Edinburgh Fringe shows have dealt with issues such as domestic violence and the US Bathroom Law, an anachronistic piece of legislation which belies a terrifying attitude towards transgender people and has had tragic consequences.

So if humour can be used as a counter-point to these kinds of issues it can also be used in a business context.

"Selling is no joke but winning is a laugh" is a concept I worked on in 2016, exploring how comedy can be put to work in business pitches and presentations.

Nevertheless in this chapter I'll be focussing more on the generic entertainment presentation – and principally how to deliver gags!

The Importance of Scripting

In a similar way to motivational presentations, where the presenter is eliciting empathy through displaying vulnerability, a script that is learned verbatim is vital in joke telling.

Almost all gags end in a punchline or word which needs to happen immediately before a "beat" or silence – the audience's cue to step in with laughter.

Getting the word order wrong, and putting the punch word anywhere but the end of the gag will have the effect of crashing or suppressing the laughter.

Compare the following renditions of the same gag:

"It's ironic as a TV that you all came out tonight to avoid watching the TV in the corner of your living room."

Versus

"You'll appreciate the irony of coming out to avoid watching television – and now you're watching a TV!"

By delaying the punch word to the end of the gag the second approach builds anticipation of the pun, and heightens the humour. Jokes have to be linguistically perfect word for word and beat for beat.

The Golden Rules of Comedy

There are three principles of good gags – Punch, Purpose and Practice.

Punch

The best jokes punch up not down. Telling a joke where Goliath is the butt is fine, but not if David is the butt. You can make a joke about the government, but not about a timid member of the electorate.

While it may be tempting to dig yourself out of a hole with self-deprecation, the humour in this varies according to different cultures. Self-deprecation is OK in the UK and tolerable in the US, but it's a complete no-no to some audiences in Asia– so know your audience!

Purpose

Not only does every joke have to have a purpose, the audience has to know the purpose as well.

Telling a joke to illustrate a point is well worth doing in all types of presentation as it enables the audience to better remember your message. Laughter and other types of "shock" allow us to access our long-term memory, so humour is very useful particularly in educational presentations.

Practice

Great jokes sound spontaneous and off-the-cuff, however this is an illusion. In order to work as well as they do they have to be meticulously practiced. Wording, pacing and timing all conspire to deliver the best gags, and the presenter needs to know them well enough to almost let them tell themselves.

In other words, the presenter will know her material so well that she won't have to think about delivering it – and instead can think about being spontaneous with the audience and enhancing the humour that way.

Make sure that your jokes tick all of these boxes and they will have most impact. But as per the usual advice, if in doubt, leave it out.

Conciseness

Jokes benefit from an economy of words. A joke or pun every 5 – 6 seconds is far more entertaining for the audience than waiting for the punch line of a long, rambling story.

When you're packing in the jokes at this rate, a five-minute presentation set can have much more impact and be more memorable than a whole hour. So keep it shorter rather than longer.

Rule of 3

The rule of 3 comes to comedy through oratory. Listen to political speeches and notice how things are grouped in threes throughout. This is used to substantiate points and add gravitas.

And of course it is the job of comedy to lampoon gravitas. The rule of 3 is a great device to set expectations and build up anticipation with points one and two, only to debunk everything with point 3.

In my set I describe some of the world's most famous drag queens – Danni La Rue, Lilly Savage…and Margaret Thatcher.

Pull back and reveal

This is a cinematic technique often used in the 'Carry On…' films, whereby the opening scene is limited in scope, presenting only a small detail of the bigger picture, and deliberately misleading the viewer. Then as the camera pans back more of the scene is revealed, causing the viewer to confront their assumptions about what they were looking at, often with hilarious consequences.

The same technique is possible in verbal as well as visual humour, such as Phil Cool's gag:

''I met my wife in Australia (limited scope opening line, conjuring ideas of love at first sight).

''I said what the bloody hell are you doing here? (This is the bigger picture, challenging the audience's assumptions.)

The next line might logically, and comically, be ''Then I saw her boyfriend'', panning out even more to give a further, more shocking reveal. But I don't think Mr Cool went that far in his version!

Tagging

The more you can build on a joke, the more mileage you can get out of it and the more jokes you can pack in to a short routine. When your sole aim is to entertain your audience and keep them laughing rather than yawning, this is a very useful technique.

Cast your eye back to the TV joke at the beginning of this chapter. It works on its own, but it's got a lot more mileage, and it's far better to get four or five laughs rather than one.

Here's how I build on it:

"Me and TV have got a lot in common.

We're both heavily made-up.

We love being the centre of attention.

Especially when we're turned on.

But the main difference is…

This TV doesn't suck."

Puns

Puns are a good source of humour and are easy to write. They rely on the ambiguity of the English language and are funny even when you've heard them before.

A lot of the humour of puns lies in the anticipation of them. Knowing the joke is coming is entertaining.

In a business context, or in private speeches, you don't have to worry about writing new material. Get a joke book. Steal other people's jokes. Just make sure you follow the Golden Rule for delivering them and remember: if in doubt leave it out.

Motivational Presentations

What are motivational presentations – and when are they useful?

There are a number of different reasons to perform motivational presentations in commercial, social and organisational terms.

If you're a sales director that needs to get more results out of your sales force you are going to have to find ways of motivating your team.

If you're representing a charity pitching for fund donations and patronage, you must find a way to tell a compelling story that will motivate your prospects to become donors.

Or you may be a CEO who wishes to change the culture of your organisation and inspire your employees towards new ways of behaving to improve communications, productivity, diversity and inclusion in the workplace.

Motivational presentations can take place in offices, in conference halls, at auditoria, during after-dinner speeches, even at workplace Christmas parties.

Certainly my own journey as Nicci began at an office Christmas Party when I wished to change the culture of my company. We had been operating under the cutthroat style of a misogynist mini-Hitler who believed under-performers had to be bullied and blamed for not delivering. In an office populated almost entirely by young, female staff, this was proving to be a wholly ineffective approach that was failing to get the best out of anyone. As a result we were losing money.

To add insult to injury the way that the operational director was treating our employees was entirely at odds with the way we were coaching our clients to behave. Our presentation team coaching is predicated on support and nurture, and while we were preaching this to our clients we were practising bullying and blaming in-house.

We were so out of integrity it hurts to think back on it. I felt for a long time that something drastic needed to be done, but it wasn't until my revered Aunt Catherine asked me how many women were on my board of directors that the penny dropped.

We needed to adopt a more feminine management style. And to get the message across I presented a motivational speech at the Christmas party, dressed as Mary Christmas, in an Anne Summers' Miss Sexy Santa costume, wig, heels and make-up.

My message was: "Stop thinking of me as your dad, start thinking of me as Mummy."

Granted it was drastic. It certainly marked a shift in attitude amongst my team, for better or worse. It definitely had an impact on the culture of the organisation, and in business terms the cross-dressing CEO managed to convert a much- needed quarter of a million pounds of sales in the subsequent three years.

So what are the Key Elements of the Motivational Presentation?

Where budget is no barrier there are typically four key elements to deploy for maximum impact. These are:

- Speech
- Media – including Images, Video and Music
- Technology
- Theatre

Let's look at each one in turn.

The Speech

*"When you can manufacture sincerity,
you've got it made."*

Groucho Marx

Whenever you have to make a speech, and especially when you are making a motivational speech, you have to be sincere. If your audience gets even a whiff of inauthenticity then you are going to crash and burn. You are certainly not going to motivate them in the way you desired.

Of course your own authentic level of emotion and passion does much to convince people of your sincerity. You must allow yourself to get emotional and perhaps to show a bit of vulnerability in order to win people over.

Although elsewhere in this book I have recommended not being tied to a script in presentations that are persuasive and educational, in the case of motivational and also entertaining presentations it is vital that you learn your speech or your script verbatim.

In the case of motivational presentations this is because you need to be emotionally exposed in order to be effective. If you are going to be emotionally exposed, you need your speech to fall back on.

Once you are comfortable with the level of emotion and vulnerability you are going to display, you then need to ensure your script fulfils the following criteria:

Build Empathy between the Audience and the Protagonist.

In the case of a motivational presentation for a charity, you need your audience to feel the pain of the protagonist, in this case the charity's beneficiaries.

Say you are fund-raising for the homeless, you might build empathy by showing images of homeless children or elderly people, and urge your audience to consider that these might be their children or relatives. To handle your audience's very human tendency towards denial, and to deal with thoughts such as "That wouldn't happen to my Dad" you might push home the point by saying "You might have thought that your Dad was OK, until the day he wandered off."

If your motivational presentation aims to get more out of your sales team, you first need your audience to identify and empathise with your organisation's sales success. As soon as they feel that the company's success is also their success, their desire will grow, and they will be motivated to engage better to ensure it.

Describe the Problem

In order to motivate people you need to be as clear and specific as possible about the problem that you need their help to solve.

For example, a homeless man can't get the medical treatment he urgently needs because he is of no fixed abode.

In the sales context, activity is low with clients and prospects opting for cheaper and better structured offers from your competitors.

Next, Describe the Solution.

Again, be as clear and specific about this. Human beings are motivated by clear and direct routes to success, so you need to show them how to get there to win their backing and support.

The sales director has to be crystal clear about how many extra calls, appointments and closures she requires over a specific time frame, and who is responsible for making them.

The charity for homeless people has a very clearly defined outreach programme – but all it needs is funding to get it off the ground and get help to the people who most need it.

Call to Action

Human nature is such that having been on an emotional journey, having identified and empathised with a problem and having been shown a clear and direct solution, we tend to want to resolve it as quickly as possible, and take action immediately to fix the issue.

If you have presented properly in an authentic way you will have the audience eating out of the palm of your hand at this point, and you need to capitalise on it. You need to give them something to do.

So you need to tell them.

In our examples here you need to either, get them to commit to doubling their sales activity, or get them to pledge money.

To galvanise them you need to get them to demonstrate their commitment. One way of doing this is to request that everyone in the audience who is prepared to commit to achieve the goals stand up. By dint of conviction, peer pressure or herd mentality, one by one all those committed will stand up and persuade their colleagues to do the same.

Close your speech by giving a round of applause for all those who committed, and giving clear instructions about what will happen next.

Finally, say Thank you.

Media

Sound and vision are emotive in a way that speech isn't. For this reason a successful motivational presentation will make optimal use of music, imagery and video to communicate its message.

There isn't really a right or a wrong way of going about this. You might use one image or a series; you might feature a piece of media that lasts between 90 – 200 seconds.

As an observation, the UK charity 'Children in Need' may have lost its audience occasionally by using video clips that are too long and too emotionally intense. Asking people to sustain a high level of emotional engagement for longer than a couple of minutes can be disempowering, leaving them feeling exhausted and helpless. This is the definition of "compassion fatigue", and it really needs to be avoided in motivational presentations.

There is a particular technique to creating motivational videos, involving either static or moving images, music that matches the images, and concise messaging, almost like poetry, which is overlaid over the images.

I prefer to use stills rather than moving images. They hold the attention better and can be zoomed in or out to enhance the effect and mood.

The text you use needs to be very tight and on message, making use of repetition and alliteration for best effect, as well as couplets and triplets to enhance the rhythm and rhyme and therefore the impact and memorability of the message.

It's important to top and tail the message also, namely ending it where you began.

Matching the music to the images and the text such that the images change on the beat, or the lyrics reflect the message results in a very satisfying presentation for the audience, enabling them to feel comfortable with what you are asking of them.

A powerful messaging technique that works really well in these types of presentation is called Bait and Switch.

First you set the Bait – a question, or a statement, which may be controversial in some way.

For example, one of our clients specialises in the fabric and infrastructure required in large, complex public buildings. Their motivational video opens with the bait statement "Constructing buildings used to be really simple."

It then goes on to debunk this statement by proving what a complex task it really is to construct functional buildings where people can work in safety and comfort.

The closing statement – how constructing buildings can be simple again – is the switch which reflects the opening bait, followed by the final Call to Action – Call us.

Technology

Beware of cutting corners in your budget for a motivational presentation. If you truly want to motivate people you have to convince them that you think the message is of the highest importance. The amount of budget you are prepared to allocate to a motivational event speaks volumes about the sincerity of your campaign.

Using the best Audio Visual technology you can afford also gives you greater control and flexibility over your effectiveness. The ability to control light and sound levels is powerful, as is a sound system with good bass, which is highly emotive.

In terms of media production technology you will want to choose a platform which gives you maximum flexibility to meld images and sounds together, for example to make things happen visually on the beat.

PowerPoint™ is a standard package but it doesn't really work in this context because it doesn't allow different media to be mixed effectively. Essentially you will achieve the maximum emotional and motivational impact if you can get the images and the text to "dance" to the music.

Theatre

The combination of your message, media and technology needs to enhance your ability to create a sense of theatre around your presentation. Audience mood and receptivity can be optimised by the simple but powerful technique of plunging the room into darkness and silence before beginning.

Relieve the darkness by spotlighting your key influencer. The first thing she says will be unforgettable after this impactful introduction.

In summary, a polished motivational presentation is all about getting all the elements right and being able to orchestrate and choreograph them together within an environment you can control.

Language of Objectives

Once you have written down your SMART objective, the language used in the objective can help you identify the type of presentation and therefore the appropriate structure.

Persuasive presentation objectives use words like *buy*, *sell*, *agree*, *commit*, *give*, and *concede*: all words that require persuasion and ultimately an element of belief. Therefore persuasive presentations are about generating belief.

Teaching presentation objectives use words like *teach*, *explain*, *understand*, and *remember* all words that require knowledge. Therefore teaching presentations are about transferring knowledge.

By analysing your objectives you can quickly determine the type of presentation, but a word of caution. Sales people always think the objective is to sell, teachers always think the objective is to teach; neither is absolute. For example if I want to sell you anti-lock brakes, I first need you to understand what they do (teach) and if I want you to learn Pythagoras' theorem I need you to see a need or application for that knowledge (sell).

Audience Objectives

Having decided on your own objectives, it is now important to consider the audience's objectives. Whilst these are perhaps secondary, it goes without saying that if we give a presentation that fails to meet their expectations, we are unlikely to achieve our own objectives. This is nowhere more important than in a marketing presentation. We have a number of clients who hold seminars or roadshows to attract new business, but if you advertise that the presentation is about learning (e.g. 'New tax rules and their implication for business owners' – a genuine example) then you had better deliver a teaching presentation before you pitch. We usually recommend that these become two different presentations, delivered by the expert who teaches and the salesperson who, after a successful training session, then stands up and does a short sales pitch. We have shown that this can be dramatically more effective than the usual 'buy our services' approach many organisations use.

Types of Presentation Structure

Once the presentation's purpose has been chosen, a presentation structure must also be determined.

Linear

This is the most common presentation structure, simply because unless you have a very small group, or you are an extraordinary presenter, presentations are by nature a linear flow of information. However, a list has little or no mnemonic properties and is not a good basis for visual structure.

Linear Structure

Developing a Visual Structure helps the audience know where they are in the presentation. We occasionally show a diagram such as this full screen, highlight the section we are about to talk about and then have the graphic shrink and move to one of the corners of the screen to act as a visual key for the information.

Hierarchy

Collins and Quillan demonstrated that presenting information in the form of a hierarchy can improve recall (Collins and Quillan, 1969). The critical issue is actually making the audience aware of this order. The diagram (overleaf) shows the visual interpretation of the structure and the ideal presentation order.

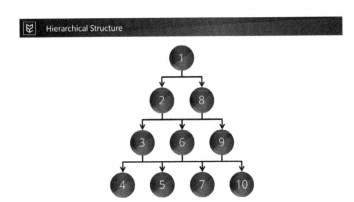

Matrix

A matrix structure can be extremely useful. Again the issue is making this structure apparent to the audience and then walking through the material in a logical sequence.

Spreading-activation models

This is proved to increase recall (Collins and Loftus, 1975). The real mnemonic benefit to using this layout comes if the audience see the building of the diagram.

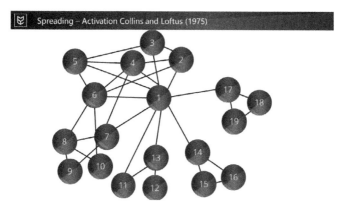

Radial

This is the one we use most (see the Value Proposition section later), five spokes giving five sections.

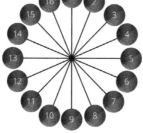

Just to be clear, I am not suggesting that these are slide layouts but presentation structures. All of them structure the information and this demonstrably helps audiences recall. Our innovation is to make the structure apparent and visual; we call this Visual Structure. The beauty of this is it helps re-enforce the message.

Chapter 9

THE ROLE OF
THE PRESENTER

———————————

Vision without action is a daydream.
Action without vision is a nightmare.

Japanese proverb

By now we have set the objectives, from this decided on a structure, produced the content and designed and animated the slides. Now for the crucial bit, the piece that brings it all together into a presentation: the presenter.

How Presenters Are:

If the dull page of bullet-points is the stereotypical bad presentation, then the unenthused, dull presenter (who reads bullet-points) is the stereotypical bad presenter.

At their best, a presenter can turn a bad presentation into a bearable one, and a great presentation into a winning one. At their worst, however, not only does the presenter add nothing to the experience (the audience can read bullet points just as quickly as they can), but they also make the process much less bearable.

Sitting on your own and reading bullet points lacks all of the depth offered by a proper winning presentation, but it is at least quicker and less mind-numbingly boring than having a monotone voice read those points to you at half speed.

Much like PowerPoint™ itself, while the presenter may be a tremendous blessing, they can also be a curse.

Role of the Presenter

In most presentations the presenter is the centre of attention. They used to be centre stage, the main flow of communication being 80% from presenter and 20% from the visual aids. Along with the shift from '*presentations with visual aids to visual presentations*' comes a shift in the balance of where the audience receives its information: from 80:20 to more like 20:80 (well, this is the aim, in reality it is probably less!).

The reasons that this is desirable have been covered at length elsewhere in the book but the psychology of it is this: we are *visual* beings – sight is our primary sense and we process visual information much faster than language.

Let me give you an example. When my son Matthew was a year old I would ask him if he wanted a banana and get no response. When he was five (if I could get his attention away from 'Bob the Builder' for ten seconds) he would pause, think about it and give me an answer.

The process is slow by comparison to my holding up a banana and asking whether he wants it. Instant response, usually affirmative both now and when he was one year old. Why the difference in response times?

At one year old he had yet to learn that the sound 'banana' was associated with the sweet yellow fruit. When he was five he knew what it meant (he could even read it) but he still had to decode the sound, remember that the word means sweet yellow fruit and then make a decision. He had to process the sound, which psychologists tell us takes longer than the visual processing that goes into seeing the fruit. We have to learn language, and that takes longer than learning what bananas taste like and whether we like them or not!

It is the same now if we are presenting to an audience in a language other than their mother tongue: say 'banana' and maybe get no response. Show a picture, everybody understands.

So if this is what we are going to do, 'show rather than tell', then the role of the presenter has to change from primary source of information (verbal) to providing supporting narrative to the visuals. This is the power of visual presenting, but it requires a complete change of behaviour for the presenter.

Again, the focus in this section is going to be on 'hard skill' changes that a presenter can make. The problems of unenthusiastic-looking presenters who struggle to make eye contact, project their voices or speak in anything but a monotone are real, but there are countless books already on that topic.

Bad habits, like reading the text, are difficult to stop, but ultimately presenting this kind of presentation is significantly easier than trying to make boring dull slides seem interesting and engaging. Whilst our approach is not necessarily easy to adopt, it certainly involves tangible, measurable changes. Most presenters take to it quickly and it becomes addictive.

Language – Precision and Clarity

Use of language is a broad topic, but some aspects are worth a mention here.

- **Jargon:** this is perhaps best described as 'professional slang', a useful device between people who know each other around an organisation, a company, etc. Yet if words are used out of context it creates problems. There may not only be a lack of understanding, but people are reluctant to ask and check. They will let the word go by and hope to pick up the gist of what is said as the presentation continues; if they do not do so, sense is inevitably diluted to some extent. What is more, it becomes more embarrassing to ask the more time goes by, and thus often less likely to happen.

- **Abbreviation:** much jargon takes the form of abbreviation, and this aspect of it is worth a mention in its own right. So much these days is reduced to initials. Of course this is often useful, but it can easily confuse or exclude people who aren't familiar with the abbreviations.

In both cases, what is being said must be checked and spelt out, at least to begin with. In business, language often links to the special nature of industries, products, organisations, processes and technology (if there is a more jargon-rife area than information technology, I cannot think of it). In every setting language must be matched to the audience. Do they, all of them, understand the kind of jargon you will instinctively use, or must you modify your language somewhat? The tone adopted must always suit the individual group to which you are speaking.

A final point about language: description is a powerful thing, or rather it can be. It is worth some thought to be sure that what you say does contain the right turn of phrase. Certainly you should avoid any bland language where something more powerful is going to have more impact: it is unlikely that anything you present in a business context should talk about something being *quite good*, or *very practical*. If there is a positive point to make, make it. Conversely, people appreciate it when things they expect to be complicated, are explained easily and quickly. It shows a confidence and expertise that assist credibility. A powerful, perhaps unusual, description is more likely to stick in the memory than something more routine. For instance, no one hearing something smooth described as: *as slick as a freshly buttered ice rink* is going to be seeing it as anything but very, very shiny, or my favourite 'The ships hung in the sky in much the same way that bricks don't' (Adams: 1979, pp. 35)

Audience focus

At any particular moment of a presentation, how do you know where your audience's attention is focused? How can you be sure that everyone is looking at the right diagram, or shifting their focus to the right areas, and at the right moment? Keeping your audience correctly focused is achieved by careful design of visual cues, building slide transitions, and ensuring the visuals do not stay on the screen for longer than necessary. If you get this right, you can hold them in the palm of your hand for as long as is necessary.

Directing Audience Focus

How well do you really know PowerPoint™?

What are the two most useful features within PowerPoint™?

At seminars when I ask this there is no single most common answer. People mention all sorts of things: being able to change the order of slides, being able to use a variety of typefaces, etc. Those most in for ridicule will say 'the ability to add clip art' as if this is somehow the panacea to all presentation ills! What is very rarely mentioned is either of our top two.

The Use of the 'B' Key

What happens in show mode (i.e. during a presentation) when the presenter presses the 'B' key? Do you know? I ask this during seminars that I have now given to probably 10,000 people. Only a handful has known, and yet I think it is probably the most important feature of PowerPoint™. Why?

Because a presentation is delivered by a living, breathing person, the contribution they make to the totality of a presentation is crucial. Sometimes the full attention of the group must be on them, on what they are saying and how they are saying it. Steps need to be taken to make this so. Press the 'B' key and the screen goes blank, so that attention necessarily must then focus on the presenter. Too often, audiences are left staring at an image on a screen that is, for the moment, irrelevant to what is being said. The facility to blank out the screen is invaluable. Press the 'B' key again and the blanked image lights up again. So simple, yet relatively few people seem to know or use it. You might also like to try the 'W' key, which turns the screen white.

The Ability to Locate a Particular Slide

I am essentially a salesperson and have spent many years 'carrying a bag' as they say in the US. Here is a scenario that has happened to me countless times.

I am in the middle of a pitch to the Marketing Director when the CEO walks in and says 'So what is this all about?' CEOs have, in my experience, many common attributes, the most significant being their attention span and their ability to influence a sale by giving their approval. If you have ever been a salesperson then you have been in this situation: you have two minutes to convince the CEO, two minutes that will probably decide the sale.

So, somewhere in your presentation you have a winning slide (see later); the slide that summarises the Value Proposition; the one slide you need to show the CEO, after which they will be interested, or not! How do you get there?

If you think that the process is 'Esc', followed by *Slide Sorter*, scroll down, double click the slide and then press *Slide Show*, then you don't really understand PowerPoint™.

You need to be familiar with your slides, but if you want to jump to, say, Slide 24, perhaps to answer a question, hit the numbers '2' and '4' and then the 'Return' key, and up comes Slide 24. Again this is an invaluable, and often little used, feature. Also try the 'Home' key for going to the first slide or the 'End' for the last slide (try pressing F1 whilst in show mode and PowerPoint™ will bring up a list of in-show commands).

To do this	Press
Perform the next animation or advance to the next slide	N Enter Page Down Right Arrow Down Arrow Space Bar
Perform the previous animation or advance to the previous slide	P Page Up Left Arrow Up Arrow Backspace
Go to slide number	number + Enter
Display a blank black slide or return to the presentation from a blank black slide	B or Period
Display a blank white slide or return to the presentation from a blank white slide	W or Comma
Stop or restart an automatic presentation	S

End a presentation	ESC
Erase on-screen annotations	E
Go to the next slide, if the next slide is hidden	H
Set new timings while rehearsing	T
Re-record slide narration and timing	R
Start the laser pointer	Press and Hold Left Mouse button for several seconds
Change the pointer to a pen.	Ctrl + P
Change the pointer to an arrow.	Ctrl + A
Change the pointer to an eraser.	Ctrl + E
Show or hide ink markup	Ctrl + M
Hide the pointer and navigation button immediately	Ctrl + H
Hide the pointer and navigation button in 15 seconds	Ctrl + U
View the **all slides** dialog box	Ctrl + S
View the computer task bar	Ctrl + T
Display the shortcut menu	Shift + F10
Go to the next hyperlink (or other hotspot) on the current slide. ("Hotspots" include hyperlinks, animation triggers, audio objects, and video objects.)	Tab
Go to the last or previous hyperlink on the current slide	Shift + Tab

PowerPoint™ is surely something that must be regarded as an essential working tool. As such, we must be familiar with it. This is especially so for sales people and their sales pitches. Most sales people are drivers (that is a comment about owning cars not a personality type, although…!). There will be few, if any, buttons on the dashboard of their cars for which they do not know the function. Maybe PowerPoint™ should be regarded in the same way.

Having described PowerPoint™ as a tool, perhaps the following analogy brings the point to life. Consider PowerPoint™ as comparable to a pencil. Most people can write and draw using a pencil. But only after some consideration and practice, and perhaps training, can they execute something more artistic. Many can 'write with it' as it were, but it contains the potential to be used as an artist would use it. You just have to know how to do so.

PowerPoint™ is surely the same. Indeed when we interview for graphics staff for our team, part of the process involves giving them a piece of paper and a pencil and asking them to sketch 'customer service'. Those that can produce something good enough to hang on the boardroom wall stay for the rest of the interview – those that don't, do not.

To the Screen

The easiest way to direct attention to the screen is to gesticulate (point to) and at the same time make something happen on the screen – an animation or build. If you also turn and look at the screen yourself (potentially breaking a traditional rule of not talking to the audience with your back to them!) you will compel them to look at the screen.

To the Presenter

This is often harder to do. First ensure that there is nothing to distract them on screen. If necessary press 'B' or 'W' to blank the screen (they almost immediately look at you!). Secondly use silence to compel their attention, nothing works better than saying nothing to make the audience stop what they are doing or thinking and look at the presenter expectantly.

Levels of Presenting

First, in preparing and delivering, the overriding consideration is the audience. Everything that is done must be audience focused. A presentation cannot consist of your saying it as you see it; rather the presenter's job is to work with an audience to help them understand the message and put things in a way designed – specifically designed in every way – to ensure that the objectives (persuasive or otherwise) are achieved.

To get it right, it helps to bear in mind that there are, in this context, three levels of presenting:

1. **Level One** presenters run in this sequence: CLICK (to bring up the next slide), read (go through what is on it – often verbatim), and explain (add to what is on it – too often leaving the slide there to distract after the relevance of what it presents has passed). Remember that people read *seven times faster than you can read out loud*.

2. **Level Two** presenters are more familiar with their presentation and will begin to explain, CLICK and show

a slide, this is much better and from the audience's point of view looks slick.

3. **Level Three** is the integrated approach: using the visualisation and the patter in a cohesive whole. The effect is best described as seamless, and if asked which contributes most – what they see or what they hear – an audience should be hard-pressed to disentangle the different elements. The best example of this is good, well-produced television.

If anything needs to be read, rather than reading verbatim it may be better to paraphrase or to reverse the words. Sometimes there are things that must, by their nature, be put over verbatim. One example of this is testimonials in a sales pitch, others might be a definition, quotation or anything where the exact wording matters.

This may not initially be easy to execute (remember the story of the New York visitor asking directions? *How do I get to Carnegie Hall? – Practise!*), but the effort is well worthwhile because this style of presenting does the most powerful job for you and marks you as a real professional. Professionalism in presenting rubs off. People then assume that you must also be expert, experienced, and capable.

Don't Read the Text

Reading text that appears on the screen is counter-productive and can distract the audience. The role of the presenter is to add value to visuals, not to clash with them. One technique we find useful is to use different words to say the same thing, for example if on screen the slide reads

'Customer Service' we would encourage the presenter to say '*We consider the most important aspect of our business to be you, the client, and servicing your needs is a critical skill for us*'. Alternatively you can produce a halfway effect by reversing the order of the words. In the example above we could just say '*Servicing our customers is extremely important to us*'.

Of course the best plan is to have no words on the screen, thus eliminating the temptation to read them in the first place. Be warned this is easy to say but difficult to do; you have to spend a considerable amount of time practising the art of reading!

To emphasise the point:

- Don't use speaker notes.
- Don't write scripts.
- Don't wear white socks.

Why? Because you will come across as an amateur!

Occasionally when presenters use a script they end up concentrating on it more than on the audience, which is a recipe for disaster. Presentations need to be dynamic and audience-centred. A script, almost by definition, prevents dynamism by compelling you to follow it. Therein lies the real problem.

When you use a script you ignore your slides, when you ignore your slides you drive a wedge between phonetic information (you) and visual information (the screen). That prevents Dual Encoding (understanding by the audience of what they hear and what they see at the same time).

Unless you are very, very, very good at presenting using a script won't work well. (A professional actor can sometimes pull it off, and some TV presenters can read an auto-cue and make it look natural, but one only needs to see the show Have I Got News for You in the UK to see the difference between a professional and an amateur.)

So why do people do it? Well, like a number of things that people do to help when they are stressed, it's easy. You have been reading since you were 3 or 4, and you can do it in your sleep (well, OK not really but it is easy). Reading is easy, and so using a script to help overcome stress is a popular approach – especially when your brain chemistry is being altered by that wonderful survival drug adrenalin.

Those that can *do*; those that can't… *read a script*.

How to Present Quotes

Nowhere is it more important to not read the text than when presenting a quote. We recommend that you follow these steps to presenting quotes effectively:

1. Slide builds with heading and client logo.
2. Explain the relevance of the quote.
3. CLICK, turn to the screen and read the quote to yourself silently. (This compels the audience to do the same plus it allows you to estimate the time needed for them to read it. They will be slower than you as this is the first time they have seen the quote.)

4. Turn to the audience and when they make eye contact (thus signalling that they have completed reading the quote) then build the reference's credibility.

You will find this a powerful way of presenting quotes.

It has often been remarked to me that surely it is OK to occasionally read text in a presentation in order to emphasise a point. Again, I feel that whilst this is right, it is the exception to the rule. I would prefer to present a quote like this:

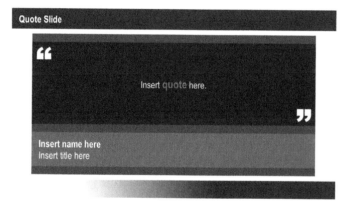

Final Details

Success is the sum of details.

Harvey S Firestone (1868–1938)

The purpose of a business presentation is to convey information to a group of people in order to educate or persuade. Everything we have talked about, (getting the message right, visualising it, designing it, rehearsing it) means nothing if we don't actually get to deliver it. Over the last 25 years as a professional presenter I have experienced every possible hiccup. I have turned up at the wrong venue, at the wrong time; I have had equipment fail or not show up, laptops crash in the middle of a presentation, projectors die half way through; you name it, it has happened to me. Most of these were not my fault. None of them prevented the presentation from going ahead (except the lack of an audience, which did throw me off my stride a little). Why? Because you learn very quickly as a presenter, or presentation organiser, to have a backup plan.

Rehearsals are vital; as is the manner in which feedback is given to the presenter.

A while ago at the Institute of Sales and Marketing I gave a presentation called "Friendly Assassins and Enemy Plants." This refers to fact that many presenters often face their biggest hurdle when they are rehearsing in front of a critical leader/boss/coach. There to help and encourage, the presenter's team often winds up breaking their spirit by nit-picking too much and failing to mention what was done well. Most people couch the feedback with, "Great (insert positive qualifier), but…" and then a list of mistakes.

What the Presenter Hears

Now from the presenter's view of the world, next time they take to their feet they will forget the positive qualifier and focus on correcting the list of mistakes. Unfortunately, this usually winds up backfiring – rather than focusing on the story or the sale at hand, the presenter preoccupied with avoiding errors.

Of course some presenters are naturally good and confident. They take negative feedback and turn it into a constructive critique that fuels a better performance. However, most people are not professional presenters and it's very hard to be positive in the face of a list of gaffs. Especially if the critique came from your Boss, or your Boss's boss.

Making Criticism Constructive

The next time you have the opportunity to provide feedback on a presentation, here's some ways to ensure your feedback has a good impact:

- Listen for the good stuff and make notes about what worked well
- Commend the presenter on cool sound bites, interactions, rhetorical questions, pauses – all the components of a great presentation
- Carefully select the areas you believe the presenter should focus on improving
- Sandwich the critique between to positive reinforcements

- Always use constructive comments – say, "it might be better if you said it like this…" rather than "Don't say that."

Providing good, positive feedback is a skill that takes practice and thought, especially for busy executives who are coaching their teams. This is the secret sauce for successful presentations though – presenters need to have confidence in their message and delivery, and who better to help them get it than the boss?

Most of our presentations get used face-to-face, either one-to-one with a laptop or one-to-many with a projector. However, we are producing more and more presentations for delivery over the web. Let us treat these separately for the moment.

Presenting Face-to-Face

By now you know your message and have a coherent presentation with the patter worked out and practised. Now comes the bit that makes a difference: bringing it together for a performance. Ultimately, that is what this is, a performance, equivalent to being on stage front and centre. That's why it is anxiety-provoking (anybody who tells you otherwise is either lying or dead). Everybody gets nervous before a presentation; the trick is to turn those nerves into enthusiasm to fuel the performance.

One-on-One

When presenting to small groups or individuals you can usually get away with using a single laptop screen. With audiences of over four it is difficult to work on a small screen and some kind of additional large screen is needed (projector, plasma, etc.) Here are some hard-earned tips for these situations.

1. Connect the laptop first, turn on the monitor and then boot up the PC, this way the PC will see the external monitor and enable it. If this doesn't work you may need to 'toggle' the screen with one of the function keys (my laptop is function F5, but they are all different).
2. Make sure that the resolution you are driving from the PC is compatible with the projection device. It is best to feed the projector its highest native resolution, which is not the highest resolution it will detect and display; but the highest resolution that it will not resize. This gives a much clearer image.

Large Meetings

1. Have a backup PC. While it is acceptable to ask one person to wait for three minutes while a PC reboots, 100 people look like a mob.
2. Test the equipment prior to the presentation (especially if you have an AV technician available).
3. Use a remote mouse if possible.
4. Make sure that people at the back can hear you (sound check) and see the screen (the bottom is usually the hardest if there are people in front of them).
5. Be strictly under time, especially at conferences. Nothing irritates people more than a presenter exceeding his

or her allotted time. If they are behind and you get them back on time, they will be grateful.

6. If you have to give your presentation to a technician to run on a PC that is not your own, make sure they have the correct version of PowerPoint™ and that it has the latest patches and security updates, otherwise it may not look or behave as you expect.

7. Breathe.

Handouts

On the whole, we don't recommend the use of handouts; controversial, I know. It has become a collective habit to print the slides three or six to a page and give it to the audience, sometimes ahead of time. I have several objections:

1. I want their attention on me or the screen and I want to be able to manipulate that attention as best I can. This is difficult if they are reading something else.

2. I want to control the pace and flow of information – again this is difficult if they can read ahead.

3. In a sales presentation the message is the most important information I have. If I print it I lose control of it, and that strikes me as counter-productive (if the CEO wants to see the presentation *I* want to deliver it, not let somebody who works for him/her present it). It is also a safe bet that as soon as you put it on paper it ends up with the competition.

4. The definition of a good PowerPoint™ slide is that it should not make sense to the audience until the presenter explains it. The printed slides probably do

not make sense, so why hand them out and leave them open to interpretation?

5. We use four dimensions to present, by giving them 2D you lose information as well as impact.

Evaluation

When we help clients make pitch presentations we are successful more than 85% of the time. Sales people who are always fixated on closing the order (at least the successful ones) tend to relax when they have the order, believing everything went OK because they won. The reality is that success hides flaws. It's easy to lose sight of how much better a presentation (or, in fact, anything) could've gone whilst the overall result is positive. This might not seem like a worry, but these slight negatives eventually add up.

I think it is important to attempt to find out what we could have done better, so we always ask for a debrief after a presentation and ask what they thought went well and what could have been done better. It is the only way to improve.

Tips for Presenting

Finally in this section some general tips for your presentations:

- If you forget what you were going to say, CLICK and move on – they won't notice.
- Know what is going to happen when you CLICK.
- Pause for effect.

- Don't apologise and never criticise your own presentation or the slides.
- In patter use a different frame of reference e.g. £1.2m per annum says '£100k each and every month'.
- Never contradict a figure.
- Round figures off in patter, e.g. 76.4% is '*about three quarters*'.

CONCLUSION

Presentation is hard.

Presenting is hard for the very reason it's worthwhile. It's a rich medium which let's us communicate in a rich way, but it also offers us many different ways to mess up. In a presentation, there's no chance to go back and fix things.

It's easy, as with all difficult things, to conclude that presenting is something that some of us can just never do. It's easy to dismiss presenting as being something innate – charisma or confidence. Whilst these may help, I hope I've been able to convince you that virtually anyone can deliver an engaging, effective, memorable presentation with only a small amount of coaching, a properly constructed presentation and a bit of practice.

I've been preaching the message of a new type of presentation for over 20 years now, and though a number of companies have changed, there's still an almost infinite number left. Death by PowerPoint is still everywhere.

The opportunity for presenters is enormous; this is a game changer for almost any of us. The opportunity for the rest of us, those sitting in the seats listening to presentations, is also huge. There's no one in business, or education, or government that couldn't have their lives improved by the time-consuming, boring and ineffective presentations that dominate being superseded by the sort of presentations that actually win.

`

ACKNOWLEDGEMENTS

I'd like to thank Matador, for their helping making this book a reality, shutterstock, for their stock images, and all the team at m62 vincis, both for their work producing presentations every week, and specifically in producing illustrations for this book.

Most importantly, I'd like to thank my wife, for her years of putting up with me.

GLOSSARY

Active Mnemonic Process – a technique used by an individual to help remember something

Animation – Digital movement (including appearance and disappearance) of objects

Animation Builds – Sequences that build up the sections of the slides to convey the message in a dynamic way

Attention Span –The length of time an audience can fully concentrate

Build Time – Time it takes between a CLICK and the end of the animation

Build up – the construction of a diagram in stages

Carrying a bag – US slang for sales activity

CLICK –The indication in this book of a click during a presentation

CLIPART – Crass Little Inserted Pictures, Always Rubbish & Trite

Closed questions – A question that is phrased so as to convey the questioner's assumption

Consultative selling – A sales process developed by Mack Hanan

Contrast –The definition of one colour shade against another.

Corporate ID – A template or set of guidelines reflecting a company's identity

PowerPoint™ Template – A file that contains the styles in a presentation

CRAVE – Mnemonic device for presentation (Chunking; Relevance; Association; Visualisation; Elaborate rehearsal)

Credibility – Trust in a person or group of people

Cue – To prompt (usually an actor)

Cue Card – List of bullet points serving as a memory aid for the presenter

Death by PowerPoint™- A presentation consisting mostly of bullet-points that are read out to the audience by the presenter. Blue background, yellow text and irrelevant pieces of Clip Art are often features.

Design – The process of deciding how a slide is laid out or looks

Directed Attention – Use of animation/build to ensure that the audience's attention is focussed on the correct part of the slide

Educational Presentation – A presentation that seeks to transfer information or skills

Empathy – the ability to understand and share the feelings of another, and the use of this to relate to them

Entertaining Presentation – A presentation exists for the enjoyment of the audience

Excel™ – A Microsoft application for creating spreadsheets

General Sales Presentation – A presentation designed to help win business that can be used at any time (isn't tailored for a specific pitch)

Handouts – information (often printouts of bullet-point slides) printed on a piece of paper given to the audience

Jargon – Professional Slang

Keying the Slide – Using visual imagery to complement the message

Legends – Explanatory labels added below a graph

M62 Vincis – My company

Medium – A means of conveying information (singular of media)

Messaging – The process of deciding a presentation's content

Microsoft Project™ Files – Project plans created in Microsoft Project

Mnemonic – A system to make remembering information easier

Motion Builds – An animation effect that moves the object in relation to the slide

Motivational Presentation – A presentation intended to elicit an emotional response

Objective Quality Standards – A list of evidence-based principles

OHP Acetate – Overhead Project Acetate, an old technology for displaying Visual Aids now only ever used to identify presenters over the age of 80

Open questions – A question which seeks understanding without putting across a questioner's assumption

Passive Mnemonic Process™ – A mimicking of an active mnemonic process to help an audience remember something

Persuasive Presentation – A presentation that seeks to convince the audience to do or agree with something

Proof – Evidence establishing the truth of a statement

Sales – helping people to buy

SMART objectives – Specific, Measurable, Action orientated, Realistic, Timed goals

Specific Sales Presentation – A presentation designed to win business in a single pitch or occasion

Spin – Giving subtly different meanings to.

SPIN™ – Patented approach to Sales

Static Build – An animation effect that leaves an object where it is in relation to the slide

Storyboard – A PowerPoint sketch of the presentation content

Strategic Selling – A sales process developed by Miller Hieman

Subjective Quality – Judgement based on an individuals' own taste and preferences

Value Proposition – An answer to two questions: 'Why would I do it?' and 'Why would I do it with you?'

Vincis – Latin for 'you win'

Visual Aid – Something for the audience to look at during a presentation

Visual Cognitive Dissonance – A Vincis concept that refers to the effect achieved by an intentional inconsistency between the visuals and the patter

Visual keys – Using visual imagery to complement the message.

Visual Segue – A Vincis concept of smooth transition in the slide

Visualisation – The process of turning text into pictures and diagram

2D Presenting – Traditional presentation style. The presenter reads static text slides to the audience.

4D presenting – The Vincis presentation method. Slides build over time with pattern integrated at the correct stages to explain the progression.

BIBLIOGRAPHY

Morley, A., Atherton, C. and Oulton, N. (2016). *Improving memory for presentation material through Visual Cognitive Dissonance: A comparison of m62 designed presentations to the "next best alternative"*. UCLAN.

Paivio, A. (1986). *Mental redundancies: a dual coding approach*. University of Ontario.

Bower, G. and Clark, M. (1969). Narrative stories as mediators for serial learning. *Psychonomic Science*, 14(4), pp.181-182.

Craik, F. and Watkins, M. (1973). The role of rehearsal in short-term memory. *Journal of Verbal Learning and Verbal Behavior*, 12(6), pp.599-607.

Bower, G.H. (1972). Mental imagery and associative learning. In L. Gregg (Ed.), *Cognition in learning and memory*, 51-88

Mayer, R. (2002). Rote Versus Meaningful Learning. *Theory Into Practice*, 41(4), pp.226-232.

Peterson, L. and Peterson, M. (1959). Short-term retention of individual verbal items. *Journal of Experimental Psychology*, 58(3), pp.193-198.

Murre, J. and Dros, J. (2015). *Replication and Analysis of Ebbinghaus' Forgetting Curve*. University of Amsterdam.

Ebbinghaus, H. (2013). Memory: A Contribution to Experimental

Psychology. *Annals of Neurosciences*, 20(4).

Murdock, B. (1962). The serial position effect of free recall. *Journal of Experimental Psychology*, 64(5), pp.482-488.

Tulving, E. and Osler, S. (1968). Effectiveness of retrieval cues in memory for words. *Journal of Experimental Psychology*, 77(4), pp.593-601.

Tulving, E (1968) *Theoretical issues in free recall*. In T.R. Dixon & D.L. Horton (Eds) Verbal Behaviour and General Behaviour Theory. Englewood Cliffs, NJ: Prentice-Hall.

Collins, A.M & Quillian, M.R (1969) *Retrieval time for semantic memory*. Journal of Verbal Learning and Verbal Behaviour, 8 240–247.

Collins, A. and Loftus, E. (1975). A spreading-activation theory of semantic processing. *Psychological Review*, 82(6), pp.407-428.

James, W (1890) *The Principles of Psychology*. New York: Henry Holt & Company.

George Doran (1981): 'There's a S.M.A.R.T. way to write management's goals and objectives'; 1981 edition Management Review

Baddeley, A.D. (1981) *The concept of working memory*. Cognition, 10, 17–23.

Baddeley, A.D. (1986) *Working memory*. Oxford University Press.

Scripts in memory for text. Cognitive Psychology, 11, 177–220